[S.S. 537]

Ia/24495

SUMMARY

OF

RECENT INFORMATION

REGARDING THE

GERMAN ARMY AND ITS METHODS.

GENERAL STAFF (INTELLIGENCE),
GENERAL HEADQUARTERS.
January, 1917.

(B16/760)   6000   1/17   H&S   4174wo

FireStep Publishing

FireStep Publishing
Gemini House
136-140 Old Shoreham Road
Brighton
BN3 7BD

www.firesteppublishing.com

First published by the General Staff, War Office 1917.
First published in this format by FireStep Editions,
an imprint of FireStep Publishing, in association with
the National Army Museum, 2013.

NATIONAL
ARMY
MUSEUM

www.nam.ac.uk

ISBN 978-1-908487-90-2

Cover design FireStep Publishing
Typeset by FireStep Publishing
Printed and bound in Great Britain

Please note: *In producing in facsimile from original historical documents, any
imperfections may be reproduced and the quality may be lower than modern
typesetting or cartographic standards.*

CONTENTS.

                           A 2

LIST OF PLATES.

SUMMARY OF RECENT INFORMATION REGARDING THE GERMAN ARMY AND ITS METHODS.

I.—DEFENCES.

1. General organization of a German position.—The general principles underlying the German defensive organization in trench warfare vary in no way from our own. Such differences of practice as are apparent, when, for instance, the trenches of the opposing forces shown on a trench map are compared, are mainly due to the greater amount of work which the enemy exacts from his troops.

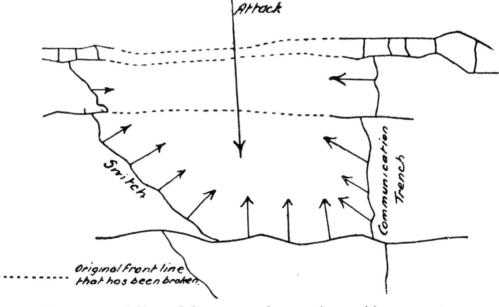

To ensure a stubborn defence, several successive positions, or systems of defence, are prepared—at least two, but more often three*; and, to prevent an enemy extending his success should he carry part of the first position, numerous switches or diagonal lines are provided.

---

* Called *Erste Stellung, Zweite Stellung, Dritte Stellung,* and generally translated as Front Line Position, Second Line Position, Third Line Position.

These not only form lateral retrenchments, but, should an enemy break in, they constitute, in combination with the back line to which they are connected, a new line of defence. Moreover, this new line is a "pocket" in which the successful enemy is exposed to heavy converging fire (*see* sketch on page 9). Thus the dangers of a break through, unless the enemy is on a very broad front and has taken measures to deal with the switches, are very much reduced.

The distance between successive positions must, in theory, be sufficient to entail fresh preparations and oblige an enemy to push forward his observation posts, and at least a portion of his batteries, before venturing to attack the second position after capturing the first. This distance naturally varies with the form of the ground, but is at least 1 kilometre. This principle does not, however, prevent the Germans from constructing minor intermediate lines and posts* on suitable ground between positions.

Hitherto each position (*see* Fig 1) has consisted of at least two continuous lines, but generally of three†—front line, support line, and reserve line, the distance between the two first being roughly from 50 to 100 yards. These lines include strong points, such as villages or woods which may happen to be situated in the forward area (*see* "Strong Points" on page 16). The present tendency is to construct not more than two lines at an increased interval of 150 to 200 yards. This interval is determined by the factor that the support line shall be far enough away not to be exposed to artillery fire directed on the front line, but yet near enough to allow the men in it to get up quickly to the latter to repel an assault or to make a counter-attack.

A circulation trench similar to our supervision or traffic trench is sometimes made behind the front line.

The distance between the support and reserve lines depends on the ground, but is not likely to exceed 800 yards.

The preparation of a support line has been advocated, even if the available forces are insufficient to admit of its occupation, as it encourages an enemy to scatter his artillery fire over a wide area. It would be, in fact, a dummy trench.

In the same way as between successive positions, switches or diagonal lines are provided between the various lines. These may be sited so as to serve as communication trenches also.

The ordinary communication trenches are, however, generally organized for defence; so that wherever an enemy breaks through the front or support trench, he finds himself in a "pocket" exposed to converging fire from three sides.

---

* Called "*Zwischen-Stellung*" and generally translated as Intermediate Position.
† *Erster Graben, Zweiter Graben, Dritter Graben,* and generally translated as First Trench, Second Trench, Third Trench.

An endeavour is made to site support lines, but not front lines, on reverse slopes, so that they may be screened from hostile ground reconnaissance and observation, and consequently be less liable to accurate artillery fire. Rear lines of defence constructed during the operations on the Somme, however, when the Germans were being gradually pressed back, were generally constructed on reverse slopes.

When driven back from one line of defences to another, the German is an adept at contesting every inch of the ground by making use of shell holes to form irregular advanced lines of defence. Should the further advance of the attackers be delayed for any time, the shell holes are joined up and a fire trench is gradually established.

2. **Trace of trenches.**—The first line is traced so as to utilize the ground to the fullest extent, and is never straight, but suitably broken with salients and re-entrants, so as to secure plenty of flanks. It is considered that the best means of holding a position is by effective flanking fire. A long field of fire is not sought for.

The general trace of the support and reserve lines, while similarly utilizing the ground, is usually straighter than that of the front line, but never lacks numerous short flanks. Care is taken not to make the support trench parallel to the front line, in order to save it from being destroyed at the same time.

3. **Design of trenches.**—The actual design of trenches in plan is similar to our own, except that the passages round the traverses are more rounded. The distance between traverses is put at 24 to 30 feet, they are made 6·5 to 13 feet thick, and project 6 to 12 feet into the trench.

The profile of the trenches is generally similar to our own, except that an elbow rest is provided, and the trench behind the fire step is usually deeper and wider. It is considered that narrow trenches with steep sides are more disadvantageous and cause more casualties—men being buried—than wide trenches, even if the latter have to be made shallow.

4. **Wire.**—One of the most distinctive features of the German defences is the labour expended on constructing thoroughly good and effective wire entanglements. Every defensive line. switch and strong point, is protected by a strong wire entanglement on iron or wooden posts, sited, if possible, so as not to be parallel to the trenches behind it. Endeavours are made to provide two or three belts, each 10 to 15 feet or more deep, with an interval between the belts of 15 to 30 feet. These intervals are filled, if possible, with trip wires, pointed iron stakes, &c., and blocked by occasional bands of entanglement connecting the belts (*see* Fig. 2).

Four different lengths of iron screw pickets are supplied, the longest, which has five loops, giving a height of 4 feet above ground. The distance apart of the pickets in an entanglement is intentionally irregular, but averages about 6·5 feet.

Knife-rests, expanding cylinders of wire, and other portable obstacles are used when it is impossible to erect posts.

A special portable obstacle, called the Lochmann entanglement, has sometimes been used. It consists of a net of barbed wire, about 13 feet wide and 180 feet long, which is unrolled and then erected on two-legged iron pickets, placed by men who crawl under the wire and peg it down at the sides.

If possible, entanglements are protected from the enemy's artillery fire by placing them in natural depressions or in sheltered trenches dug for the purpose. This is to be expected in the second and third positions, rather than in the front system.

5. **Saps.**—One special feature of the German trench system is the large number of listening "saps" (*see* Fig. 1) run out in front of the line. They are often executed by actual sapping. After a number of them have been pushed forward a certain distance, cross heads may be made. These are then extended towards each other, and a new trench is in time formed closer to the enemy.

Listening posts are also formed in shell craters and specially constructed holes, reached by tunnels and situated beyond the wire.

6. **Revetments.**—Although a great deal of timber is seen in revetments, it is laid down that, if possible, planks, baulks and other material which is likely to block a trench and interfere with traffic if a trench is shelled, should not be employed for this purpose. Hurdles are permissible, but the most suitable revetments are considered to be well-built sods or thin brushwood laid loose behind stout well-anchored pickets; rabbit wire is, however, used to a considerable extent. Sandbags, as with us, are only to be used for rapid work and urgent repairs, or in localities where the ground necessitates the employment of breastworks.

7. **Drainage.**—Great attention is paid to the drainage of trenches, as on the success or non-success of the measures taken may depend whether the position can or cannot be held in the wet season. It is laid down that the drainage must be done on a definite plan which must be carried out in good time. Drainage engineers and geologists are to be consulted, and use made of existing maps and plans. Whenever possible, the drainage water is to be led in the direction of the enemy, pipes being put through the parapet for this purpose. On high ground, when drainage is simple, keeping the trenches in good order, gutters in the sole of the trench, sump holes and keeping the ordinary ditches and water channels clear are considered the usual measures to be taken. In low ground, it may be necessary to lower the water level of the whole sector by elaborate pumping installations at a distance from the trenches. Otherwise, the water in the trenches is pumped or baled into pipes leading towards the enemy.

Special care is taken to keep surface water out of the trenches by cutting channels to divert it or by running it over the trenches, towards the enemy, in pipes.

8. **Observation posts and sentry posts.**—The German bullet-proof shield can be used either as a loophole, or for observation, the loophole cover being designed so that, if desired, only a narrow slit of the opening can be exposed. It is laid down that shields are only necessary for sentries; to meet an attack, all firing must be over the parapet.

Observation posts are of various patterns: for direct vision (with or without overhead cover), for mirror observation, and for periscope observation. In the last case, the emplacements may be entirely of ferro-concrete with only a small hole in the roof for the instrument to pass through (*see* Fig. 3), or the observation post may be merely a timbered shaft (*see* Fig. 4). Steps leading to dug-outs below may be found even in substantial concrete observation posts.

With mirror observation, the observer stands to one side of the loophole with the mirror placed in the same horizontal plane as the eye so as to reflect what is outside the loophole. Single rifles and rifle batteries are fired from cover in a similar way by means of a mirror attached to the rifle or rifle stand.

9. **Dug-outs.**—Immense energy has been shown by the Germans in the construction of shell-proof dug-outs and in the protection of their weakest point, viz., the entrances.

Except in breastworks, when they are inevitable, shelters under the parapet are seldom used. When they are employed it is suggested that they should be of ferro-concrete, so that there is little chance of their collapsing and bringing down the parapet. Entrances to deep dug-outs are, however, almost invariably found under the parapet, opening into the fire trench, so that the entrance may be as little as possible exposed to fire, and the passage down and the dug-out itself may have the benefit of the extra earth cover offered by the parapet. This cover is supplemented by a layer of concrete or rails.

Fig. 5 shows the usual plan of a deep mined dug-out. The tendency is to construct these dug-outs on a uniform pattern in order to ensure economy of time and material, and to make it easier for new troops to find their way about them.

In many cases the dug-out has two floors, the upper one, being better ventilated, serves as living quarters, the lower one as a secure refuge in case of intense bombardment (*see* Fig. 6). The entrance to the steps leading down to the lower floor has been found carefully disguised by cloth coloured to imitate earth.

10. **Battle headquarters.**—Battle headquarters are often in a very elaborate series of dug-outs, with observation posts of various kinds, telephone rooms and every convenience.

11. **Machine gun emplacements.**—Drawings of a large number of concrete machine gun emplacements have been captured, but few of them have actually been seen. The regulation type has solid walls of ferro-concrete, 2 feet 8 inches thick, and overhead cover of 1 foot of ferro-concrete and two layers of 8-inch joists. This, not allowing for earth used as concealment, only exposes 3 feet 4 inches of the emplacement above ground when the sill of the loophole is at ground level.

The interior dimensions are about $7\frac{1}{4}$ feet by $8\frac{1}{2}$ feet. The gun requires a platform $3\frac{1}{3}$ feet wide and $5\frac{1}{2}$ feet long.

Theoretically, concrete emplacements are only built in back lines and where they can be concealed in woods or behind a rise of ground. They are sometimes hidden in a flank, behind a continuation of the main parapet which covers them from view from the front (*see* Fig. 7). It is recognised that in regular trench systems, the accurate trace of which is known to the enemy by aeroplane photographs, it is useless to build emplacements in the front and even the support trenches, and that the machine guns can only be kept in a serviceable condition if protected in deep dug-outs with several exits, whence it is possible to get them quickly to the parapet. These dug-outs are placed under the front parapet and sometimes have passages leading under the trench to open emplacements behind the parados, or, in some instances, well to the front of the parapet (*see* Fig. 8 and 9).

When the ground permits, emplacements are made on commanding points in the support and reserve line, which have a view over the front line. Such emplacements may be merely holes in the ground without any parapet (as illustrated in " Notes for Infantry Officers on Trench Warfare ").

It may be noted that when a machine gun emplacement is sited in a flank and fires over the entanglement, the wire immediately in front of the gun will usually be lower than in the rest of the belt (*see* Fig. 7).

In some cases, a ferro-concrete " funkhole " under the parapet of the trench, in which crew and gun can take shelter, has been provided (*see* Fig. 10).

12. **Trench mortar emplacements.**—These differ little from our own patterns (*see* Fig. 11). Alternative emplacements and observation posts, together with good cover for the gun crew, men resting, and ammunition, are provided in connection with them. The Germans frequently site their trench mortar emplacements close to light railway or trolley lines, with a view to moving the mortars rapidly from one emplacement to another,

13. **Gun emplacements.**—In theory, concealment of the guns is sought rather than their protection by covered emplacements (for methods adopted, *see* under "Concealment," on page 17). In one document it is stated that the overhead cover is merely harmful unless it is sufficiently thick to keep out a 9·2-inch shell, for the collapse of the roof may damage the gun, and cover, if destroyed, takes a long time to repair. It is better, therefore,

to trust to splinter-proof cover or concealment. If a covered emplacement is built, a wide arc of fire cannot be expected. In any case, very little timber should be used in emplacements in order to avoid danger of fire. Batteries are sometimes sited in the open without any emplacement and close to an existing road or path (in order to avoid making tracks to the guns).

In practice, at any rate on some parts of the front, the tendency is to provide cover, and as far as can be judged from aeroplane photographs, this cover is being made heavier and heavier.

Thick ferro-concrete or other cover, sufficient to resist a 6-inch howitzer is provided in the usual forms for observation posts, gun crews and ammunition. The order of work is: observation posts, cover for gunners and ammunition, and lastly for the gun itself. Special cover for men resting and reserve ammunition, is built at a little distance from the battery.

In a few instances a gun has been kept under cover in a tunnel or a hill side, and run out on rails to fire.

If the guns are in open pits, as much cover as possible is got without throwing up a high parapet. It is laid down that gun pits should be at irregular intervals, but they seldom are.

A plan of a battery and section of an observation post are given in Figs. 12 and 13.

14. **Snipers' posts.**—The ordinary German system of sniping is to detail a sniper to a certain section of trench rather than to station him at a definite post or particular loophole. On the beat thus allotted, a number of loopholes are prepared, any or all of which may be used by a sniper during his tour of duty. This multiplication of loopholes is favoured as it gives an enemy a large number to keep under observation, without requiring many snipers to man them.

The normal German sniper's post is merely a stoutly framed, rectangular, wooden sentry box, about 6 feet high and 4 feet square inside, placed in a recess in a parapet. It has a roof of planks, corrugated iron, steel rails or plates, with earth on top. On the enemy's side of the sentry box there is no boarding immediately under the roof, and a steel box-loophole projects. The sides of this box are set at about 45 degrees, and the top slopes down from about 21 inches to $7\frac{1}{2}$ inches at the front, leaving a loophole about $7\frac{1}{2}$ inches high by 2 inches wide. Leathern padded clamps to hold a rifle, capable of adjustment in both a vertical and a horizontal direction, are provided in the box. If they cannot be concealed in the parapet or in a saphead, the boxes are covered with earth so as look like small mounds. In summer they are not difficult to detect, as a shot from them disturbs the dust near.

Other posts are formed by using the ordinary steel loophole plate lodged among sandbags in the parapet, and by crude loopholes built up of two heaps of sandbags with a board or steel plate across them and a few more bags on top of it.

Loopholes are also cut in trees and stumps. Sometimes they are single, sometimes double, the upper one being used in summer when the grass is high in No Man's Land.

Some ingenuity is shown in concealing loopholes in a parapet by throwing casually on to it any object, from a tin to a ploughshare, that will hide or cast a shadow over the orifices. Coils of wire in particular have been employed for this purpose. Coloured sandbags are freely used to confuse observers.

As regards sniping during a battle, the Germans on the Somme occasionally left regular snipers behind when the garrison of a trench was withdrawn. Cases also occurred, after a trench had been overrun, of individuals taking up positions in shell holes and doing as much damage as possible before surrendering.

When an advance on our part was checked, regular snipers usually made their appearance in front of the enemy's lines, *e.g.*, in shell holes, in some of which steel plates and rations were afterwards found.

Trained snipers were quick at recognising an officer if dressed as such.

15. **Communication trenches.**--Communication trenches are very numerous. In plan they are generally curved, sometimes zig-zagged, less often traversed or elbowed. In theory, there should be two in each company sector, from the reserve to the front line, but usually there are fewer between the reserve and support lines, than from the support line to the front line. The points where they cross the support line must not be opposite to each other. The points where they enter a trench from in front are arranged for defence, the junction often being prepared as a strong point with wire all round, and loopholed traverses and bombing trenches. Wire blocks and pitfalls are placed in the trench itself.

The communication trenches are usually broader and deeper than our own, and the sides are more sloping. As they are so frequently destroyed, they are not revetted unless absolutely necessary.

Blinded communication trenches are rarely used, as splinter-proof material is no protection from heavy shells, and only serves to increase the block in the trenches if it is struck.

In some situations, very exposed to enfilade fire, a series of cover trenches have been made instead of a communication trench, the troops moving above ground by specified beaconed-out routes, and taking refuge in the trenches if shelling is commenced.

16. **Strong points.**--Great use has been made by the Germans of natural strong points, such as villages, farms, and woods. In the case of villages, the borders and interior have been strongly organized, generally for all round defence, and a particularly desperate resistance has been

offered in them. The normal procedure now, when taking up a new position, is to fix on a general line of natural strong points, and to prepare these for defence first and then to join them up by fire trenches, without much regard to the field of fire of the latter. The first indication that a new line is being constructed usually is the appearance of trenches covering villages and woods.

The system adopted by the Germans in defending villages is of the greatest importance from the point of view of the attacker. Captured orders show that they rely, firstly, on the garrison of the trenches situated in front of the villages, and secondly, on a garrison specially told off and stationed in rear of the locality. The latter garrison may be employed either for counter-attack or to occupy the defences of the village itself when the attacker has approached so near that it is impossible for him to use his artillery against it any longer. Artificial strong points are made by joining up existing trenches in suitable ways for all round defence. Isolated strong points are very rare, though well wired gun emplacements not in use by the artillery are sometimes utilized by infantry and machine guns for defensive purposes.

17. **Concealment of defences.**—Great trouble is taken by the Germans to conceal their gun positions, trench mortar emplacements, tracks, &c., whenever this is possible, in order to prevent them being conspicuous on aeroplane photographs or visible to aeroplane observers.

(*a.*) *Concrete works.*—To conceal concrete works, mortar is plastered on the surface before the cement has set, and on this, moss or roots and weeds are thrown and stamped in on the chance of their growing. In some cases the concrete has merely been painted with large irregular patches of different colours: unless this is skilfully done, however, the results are not very successful, judging by aeroplane photographs.

(*b.*) *Trenches and excavations.*—Sharp angles, steep slopes, straight lines in parapets, digging on conspicuous points, and exposure of spoil from excavations are avoided if possible.

(*c.*) *Communication trenches.*—When it is necessary to conceal communication trenches in order to escape bombardment, they are either tunnelled at 15 to 20 feet below the surface, or are merely disguised by covering them with netting on which straw, branches, &c., are placed, the whole being covered with sods or a sprinkling of earth.

(*d.*) *Roads and approaches.*—The approaches to observation posts, machine gun and trench mortar emplacements are covered or concealed, while conspicuous tracks are made to dummy emplacements.

When roads visible to the enemy have to be masked by erecting screens, other screens are erected at various distances from the road, on the enemy's side, so as to deceive artillery observers.

(*e.*) *Gun emplacements.*—It is laid down that guns should be sited in gun pits at irregular intervals. They should be connected by trenches which should be continued well out on either flank, not only for the sake of defence by rifle fire, but to give them, as far as possible, the appearance of an ordinary trench.

It is laid down that great care must be taken to conceal gun pits from aircraft during construction, when it is very likely that the newly thrown up earth may disclose their position.

If no screen or matting is erected over the gun, plenty of brushwood is kept handy to throw over it on the approach of an aeroplane.

When gun pits are made in woods, only the absolutely necessary amount of clearing is done, and wires with branches or small fir trees attached, &c., are hung over the gun. The tracks leading to the gun pits are similarly concealed.

(*f.*) *Dummy gun positions.*--The Germans make considerable use of dummy gun positions near the occupied emplacements, and employ dummy flashes in them.

(*g.*) *Dummy trenches.*—It has been found unnecess ly to dig dummy trenches more than 20 inches deep ; provided the edges ie kept sharp, it is said that they throw sufficient shadow to appear like re t ones in aeroplane photographs.

(*h.*) *Dummy saps.*—In chalky ground dummy sap are sometimes made by turning over the top soil and exposing the chalk, a small T-head being constructed at the end of the "sap" and lightly wired.

18. **System of construction of defences.**—During the battle of the Somme, the Germans prepared fortified lines of defence behind successive gaps made in their line with notable rapidity.

This rapidity appears to have been due to the following chief causes :—

(*a.*) Methodical work.
(*b.*) Practical designs.
(*c.*) Full use made of specialists.
(*d.*) Continuous hard work of the troops.

The method of distribution of work followed certain definite rules. The front to be defended was divided into sectors approximately the equivalent of a regimental sector. A complete regiment échelonned in depth was allotted for the work. By this means the troops worked on trenches which they would probably have to hold.

The dislocation caused by reliefs was minimized by the reliefs all coming from the same unit. This dislocation was still further reduced by the supervision of a specially selected officer from the regiment, who was responsible for the execution of the whole of the defences. In the case of rear lines of defence, the supervising officer was an engineer officer.

At each relief a detailed statement showing work done, work outstanding, tools available, material available, &c., was handed to the incoming unit.

Engineer stores were always dumped at the refilling places for ammunition and rations. The troops thus always knew where to go for these stores.

Carriers were found by forming a 4th platoon in each company, which was exclusively employed on carrying stores and rations.

For specialized work, specialists were grouped together into squads or groups, *e.g.*, *Betontrupps* for the construction of concrete machine gun emplacements and observation posts, and *Stollenbaukommandos* for the construction of deep dug-outs.

All work was allotted to the troops as tasks which they had to complete before being relieved.

Works in rear of the front line of defence were constructed by pioneers, Landsturm, Russian prisoners, and also by civil labour under military supervision.

II.—MINE WARFARE.

1. **Inception of mine warfare.**—Since the end of 1914, when underground activity, which plays an inevitable part in all phases of "fortress warfare," was first marked by the firing of offensive mines by the enemy, German mining policy has generally been aggressive.

The development of our own tunnelling operations, however, enabled us to give the most important sectors of our line underground defence and upon several occasions to adopt offensive measures against strong points on the enemy's front. This activity eventually dominated the enemy's policy and forced him to adopt systematic defensive mining, especially round his salients, wherever the lines were close; but he has always kept in view the possibilities of driving an offensive mine under our trenches, even when not associated with infantry operations.

2. **Influence of soil.**—The enemy's mining policy and methods, like our own, are governed by the class of soil or rock encountered. North of the La Bassée Canal, work is entirely in sand and clay, and is generally so silently performed that it can only be identified when galleries are in close proximity. To the south of the canal, work is almost wholly in chalk and is comparatively noisy, the sound of picking being audible, at times up to 100 yards, with a mine-listening instrument.

3. **Detection of mining activity.**—Valuable data may occasionally be obtained by surface observations. In the clay areas, evidence of blue clay, in dumps or disclosed in torn sandbags, and, similarly, in the chalk areas, significant enemy chalk dumps may be taken as signs of mining. Observation of working parties carrying timber or wooden cases to certain points, at certain intervals of time, indicating periods of mining reliefs, observation of fumes arising from mine entrances after a mine is fired, and the sound of pumps or windlasses heard by patrols, have afforded useful guidance to the detection of mining operations.

The enemy frequently attempts to advance by mining from the near lip of a crater; such opportunities can be denied to him by the watchfulness of our patrols and advanced posts.

In order to obtain information regarding our mining, the enemy may raid trenches where he suspects that mining is in progress, the raiding party being accompanied by tunnelling personnel.

Mine shafts sometimes have signboards, marked *Schacht* or *Stollen*. Their entrances are similar to those of dug-outs, but are usually distinguished by ventilating apparatus or some device to assist in the evacuation of spoil being fixed to the timbers. A German mine usually commences with an incline, which terminates in a chamber from which a vertical, or almost vertical, shaft is sunk. The depth of the system will vary with the nature of the ground and the scheme in hand. The enemy, like ourselves, locates the entrances to his mine system in the support trenches, or even further back.

4. **Hostile tactics prior to blowing a mine.**—Prior to an attempt to destroy a sector of our trenches, the enemy will endeavour to induce our troops to concentrate in the danger area, either by the use of decoy patrols or by bombardments on either flank of the mine area.

5. **Craters for tactical purposes.**—Mines blown by the enemy near, or even within his own lines, are at times attributed to nervousness when, in reality, they form a deliberate factor in his scheme of defence. The enemy, especially in chalk areas, has indeed frequently shown great enterprise in co-ordinating his mining policy with the demands of the tactical situation. Although the majority of his mines are fired for destructive reasons, to damage our defensive mines or to check our offensive, many are fired for " constructive " reasons. His craters may be formed to provide dominating observation over our lines, to give defilading protection to his own, or to form screened machine gun emplacements for enfilade fire. He has taken advantage of the fact that while, in the early days of mine fighting, mine craters were rare and intense artillery fire was generally concentrated upon them, they are to-day very common occurrences and may be converted, without particular danger, into valuable assets as strong points, observation posts, sites for deep dug-outs, and even assembly places for raids and minor attacks.

6. **Commanding observation.**—The enemy's offensive mines have occasionally been employed to blow back, step by step, the near lips of a crater system, from which we hold commanding observation, on high ground. This aim involves the enemy in a very active mining policy, which can only be checked by vigorous counter-mining perhaps at two levels. When the underground fighting becomes particularly vigorous and when our miners appear to have gained a decided advantage, the enemy will sometimes raid our mine heads with a view to destroying them or throwing back work, by firing mobile charges. If the raiders are only in brief occupation, the damage effected is usually insignificant, but if, on the other hand, the enemy is not evicted before he has had time to explore our mining system and destroy selected points, our loss may be serious.

7. **Significance of the enemy's mining.**—During 1916 the enemy has fired 700 mines, but, owing to our defensive systems, only a very small percentage of these, through the element of surprise, inflicted serious casualties on our infantry or occasioned any marked change in the tactical situation.

8. Organization of craters for defence.—The German method of organizing craters for defence depends largely upon their situation with regard to the existing defences of both sides. Speaking generally, however, it appears to be as follows :—

Starting from the nearest point in his line, or rather the point from which, having regard to the tactical situation, the crater can be most conveniently absorbed into the existing defences, the enemy saps towards the crater he intends to organize, digging a trench behind the near* lip. This gives him a commanding situation and makes good the interior of the crater. From here he gradually carries the trench round the crater, keeping, however, on the inside of the far* lip in order to avail himself of the natural parapet which it provides. Having thus seized the crater, if the position is considered of value he may elaborate the defensive organization by constructing "mined dug-outs," &c., near the bottom of the crater below the far* lip.

In the case of a group of craters, he usually organizes the most convenient crater in the manner described above, and then, sapping from the point nearest to the next crater, he continues the trench inside the far* lip of the latter, and so on (*see* sketch).

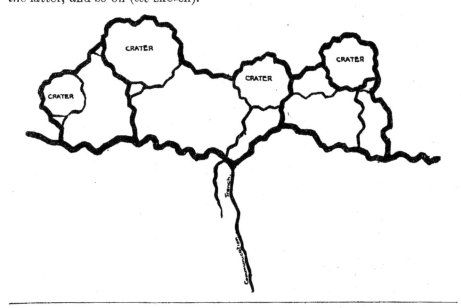

---

* The terms "near" and "far" have reference to the German line, the near lip being the one nearest to that line.

He thus forms a continuous trench inside the far* lips of the craters, and eventually joins it to the front line system. Direct communication is then provided by constructing communication trenches from the craters to the existing front line. In some cases, the defensive organization is further elaborated by the construction of a tunnel connecting the craters and roughly parallel to the trench inside the far* lips, but nearer to the German line. The trench is then connected to the tunnel by passages.

When the front line has been destroyed by mine explosions, a new trench is dug in rear of the craters and joined up to the nearest communication trench or trenches. Short connecting trenches are then made from the new trench to the craters, to provide easy access. The new trench is organized for defence and is available as a support line should the craters be retaken.

---

* The terms "near" and "far" have reference to the German line, the near lip being the one nearest to that line.

III.—MEANS OF COMMUNICATION.

A.—THE TELEPHONE.

1. **In normal trench warfare.**—Owing to the introduction of "listening sets" (*see* page   ), the use of the telephone for important messages from the front has been considerably reduced, at all events as regards messages which are sent "in clear," but the telephone systems have nevertheless been largely extended during the later phases of trench warfare.

The main points on which the Germans lay stress are :—

(*a*.) The use of metallic circuits near the front.

(*b*.) The duplication of routes whenever possible.

(*c*.) Cables should be buried at a considerable depth, viz., 10 feet across open country and 6 feet beneath the sole of a trench.

(*d*.) Large stocks of spare parts should be kept in dug-outs.

(*e*.) A system of linemen to carry out repairs should be organized.

(*f*.) The necessity for frequent tests; every half hour by day and every 13—15 minutes by night, for lines which are used for calls for barrage fire.

(*g*.) Telephone operators should be considered as being on sentry duty, and any neglect of duty should be punished from that standpoint.

2. **During a battle.**—From captured documents it is evident that most of the telephone lines near the front were cut during the preliminary bombardment at the opening of the battle of the Somme. Telephone lines further back also suffered, especially in or near villages, General von Stein (Commanding A Group, 1st German Army) summarized what were considered the essentials in telephone construction for battle purposes as follows :—

"Exposed telephone lines should be laid only far behind the front line if possible, never in front of the 3rd Line Position; even in rear of this position they should be replaced by buried cables in those villages which, on account of the proximity of a railway station, &c., are liable to bombardment by heavy artillery. In front of the 3rd Line Position, buried cable (armoured cable) should be laid at a depth of 10 feet across open country and 5 to $6\frac{1}{2}$ feet when beneath the sole of a trench provided with trench boards.

"The construction of the cable trenches must be concealed as much as possible from the enemy (work to be carried out by night or in misty weather), and trenches covered up so as to conceal them from aeroplane observation). The routes of the cable trenches must be marked on the ground by stone slabs and recorded on maps which can be given to the repair detachments.

"Telephonic communications alone, however carefully they may be constructed, are not sufficient. Several means of communication must always be available."

Another German Commander lays stress on the value of establishing permanent telephone parties in dug-outs along the lines; it is the duty of these parties to test the lines frequently and maintain them in working order.

"The usual practice of changing telephone apparatus when reliefs were carried out proved to be a source of very marked interruption, and should not take place heavy during fighting."

B.—WIRELESS TELEGRAPHY.

1. **Methods of employment.**—Wireless is employed in the German Army in three more or less distinct systems, viz. :—

(*a.*) High-power field stations.
(*b.*) Trench sets.
(*c.*) Aeroplanes.

2. **High-power field stations,** situated at General Headquarters and the Headquarters of Armies, &c., have not been much used during the past year, presumably owing to the completeness of the systems of telegraph and telephone lines in the back areas.

3. **Trench sets,** on the other hand, are now largely employed, though they were practically non-existent on the British front prior to June, 1916. Before that date, the Germans employed some of their field sets for "jamming" our aeroplane and trench set wireless, but they never seriously interferred with our work.

The necessity for some form of light wireless set, to replace the ordinary means of communication in the front area, was repeatedly urged by the German Higher Commanders after their experience of the first weeks of the Somme battle.

Their representations were successful, and at the beginning of September, 1916, the enemy began to employ trench sets for communication purposes, with the result that the activity of the German "jamming" stations almost entirely ceased.

The number of trench sets now working in the Somme area is steadily increasing, and most Divisional Sectors have at least one forward station.

4. **Aeroplane sets.**—Since the Summer of 1915, when the enemy began using wireless from aeroplanes employed in ranging artillery, he has steadily augmented and perfected this method of observation.

The use of machines fitted with wireless is not confined to the artillery flights, but wireless is also freely used by reconnaissance and counter-battery machines, and to a certain extent by "infantry aeroplanes" (*see* page 28).

C.—LIGHT SIGNALS.

1. **Types employed.**—The Germans employ the following methods of sending light-signals :—

> (*a.*) Light-pistols.
> (*b.*) Rockets.
> (*c.*) Lamp signals.

2. **Light-pistols.**—With these pistols, which are similar to our "Very light" pistols, cartridges producing various coloured lights are used. These lights are either in plain colours or some colour which eventually breaks into "pearls," "showers," &c.

They are chiefly employed for intercommunication between infantry and artillery, as signals for barrage fire, or for informing the artillery as to the necessity of lifting its fire; they are also used for warnings of gas attacks, &c.

The allotment considered necessary for a company in front line is six pistols, with a large stock of ammunition.

The code used in light-signalling is at the discretion of Corps, and sometimes of Divisions, and is subject to constant alteration.

3. **Rockets** are used in much the same way as light-pistols.

4. **Lamp signals.**—The tendency, resulting from the experience of the Somme battle, is to increase the establishment of lamp signalling detachments. General von Armin reported in August, 1916, as follows:—

"It is considered urgently necessary that a complete light-signal detachment should be formed in each Corps. A total of about 30 signal lamps of medium range is required to enable a signal line to be established for every infantry regiment and every artillery group. Besides these, four light-signal sections, with apparatus of a greater range, are required to establish long distance light-signal communications in the Divisional Sectors. . . . . The great value of communication by light-signalling was made doubly clear by the continual interruptions of the telephone communications."

In addition to the above, a special issue of signal lamps is contemplated for purposes of communication between infantry in front line and "infantry aeroplanes" (*see* under "F.—Aeroplanes" on page 27).

Various types of lamps are used, viz., oil, electric and oxy-acetylene flash lamps, for sending Morse signals, and plain lamps of various colours which are merely displayed.

D.—FLAG SIGNALS.

Flag signals are chiefly employed as substitutes for light-pistol signals when these are not available. The flags mostly used are white, red, black, or yellow flags in frames, which are waved from side to side or are merely displayed.

E.—CARRIER PIGEONS.

During the battle of the Somme, the Germans obtained very satisfactory results from carrier pigeons, which often proved the quickest means of communication. In spite of the heaviest fire, pigeons covered distances of 6 or 7 miles in 15 to 20 minutes, and reports apparently reached their destinations in nearly all cases.

The Germans also use carrier pigeons for sending messages from aeroplanes which are not fitted with wireless.

F.—AEROPLANES.

1. **Allotment of "Infantry Aeroplanes."**—In the later phases of the Somme battle, the Germans introduced the system of allotting an "Infantry Aeroplane" to each Division, with the object of conveying information from the troops to commanders.

2. **Method of work.**—The main duty of this infantry contact patrol is to keep the commander posted as to the progress of events in the front line. To assist the aeroplane in determining the position of the front line, the infantry are instructed to mark it by means of white linen strips (red when snow is on the ground), 1 foot 8 inches to 3 feet 3 inches square, as soon as the contact patrol signals his presence by means of coloured light-signals. When the contact patrol has completed his task, he sends a signal to that effect, and the strips are removed.

The contact patrol records his observations on a prepared map and, if possible, by means of photographs. Reports are submitted to the staff concerned by dropping written reports, by sending wireless messages, or by personal report immediately after landing.

3. **Use of signalling lamps.**—The above method of marking the line by strips is only a temporary expedient, and it is intended to use light-signalling lamps for this purpose when a sufficient supply is available.

4. **Tactical information.**—In addition to reporting the position of the front line, infantry aeroplanes are intended for transmitting requests for reinforcements, &c., from units in front line to battalion commanders when other means of communication have completely broken down.

These requests are sent by a pre-arranged code of lamp signals to the aeroplane, which transmits them by wireless to stations in rear.

5. Distinguishing marks of " Infantry Aeroplanes."—These aeroplanes carry a narrow, black, white and red pennon, $4\frac{1}{2}$ feet long, attached to the tail of the machine. They also attract the attention of their infantry by sounding a horn.

G.—MESSENGER DOGS.

The Germans have been experimenting with messenger dogs, the German sheep-dog being used for the purpose. Training schools have been formed and messenger dogs are now being employed in a considerable number of units.

Messages are carried in a tin box or a satchel fastened to the dog's neck.

The dogs of the 2nd Guard Division are believed to have done useful work as messengers in the fighting of the early part of September, but the results were sometimes disappointing.

The following are the main items in the dog's training :—

(1.) Absolute obedience.
(2.) Carrying a message and returning by a definite route.
(3.) Being broken to shell fire ; this is done by means of bombs.
(4.) Training not to bark.
(5.) Moving across country during a bombardment, making use of shell holes and other cover.

H.—RUNNERS.

" When all others fail, the runner still remains as the last means of communication."

The following are the main conclusions regarding runners reached by the Germans after their experience in the battle of the Somme :—

(a.) Numerous runners should be trained to know the ground; they should be picked men.
(b.) Relays of runners should be established at a normal distance apart of 100 metres, dug-outs being constructed at intervals along the routes used.
(c.) Runners should never be sent out singly, and all important information and orders should be sent in duplicate.

IV.—ARMAMENT AND EQUIPMENT.

A.—ARTILLERY.

1. **Guns in common use.**—The 7·7-cm. field gun, the 10·5-cm. light field howitzer, and the 15-cm. heavy field howitzer are the weapons with which the greater part of the German artillery is equipped. Some of the particulars of these guns are given in the following table, in which several others of the commoner types are included:—

Gun.	Calibre.	Weight of high-explosive shell.	Maximum percussion range.
	inches.	lbs.	yards.
3·7-cm. revolver gun	1·46	1·0	3,280
7·7-cm. field gun	3·03	14·5—15·5	9,186
9-cm. field gun (old pattern)...	3·46	16·5	7,109
10·5-cm. light field howitzer...	4·13	34·5	7,655*
10-cm. gun	4·13	39·5	11,264
12-cm. gun	4·73	36	7,984
13-cm. gun	5·31	88	15,748
15-cm. heavy field howitzer	5·89	86—93	9,296
21-cm. mortar (howitzer)	8·30	183—262	10,280†

* The usual maximum range is 6,890 yards, the charge for the longer range being used only in exceptional circumstances.

† The usual maximum range is 9,733 yards, the charge for the longer range being used only in exceptional circumstances.

2. **Long range guns.**—A recent feature of German artillery development has been the increasing use of long range guns, which are usually on railway mountings. The majority of these are naval guns, apparently not of the latest pattern; the calibres used against the British front include 15-cm., 24-cm. and 38-cm.

The 15-cm. naval gun is the most frequently employed, an ordinary high-explosive shell being used at ranges up to 13,000 yards, and a high-explosive shell with false cap at longer ranges. The maximum range hitherto reported is 18,700 yards.

The 24-cm. naval gun also fires two types of shell, viz., a high-explosive shell with false cap and an extremely tapered high-explosive shell, which latter is a further development of the false cap type. The maximum range hitherto reported is 27,500 yards.

The 38-cm. naval gun has occasionally been employed against the British front, firing a high-explosive shell with false cap.

3. Field artillery ammunition.—The most noteworthy recent changes in connection with the ammunition of the German field artillery are the following:—

(a.) The abolition of the "universal shell" for both field gun and light field howitzer.

(b.) The abolition of the 1896 and 1914 patterns field gun shell and the 1914 pattern light field howitzer shell, all of which have very small bursting charges.

(c.) The introduction of a "long shell" for the field gun (high-explosive bursting charge, 2 lbs.). A "long shell" for the light field howitzer has been in use for some time, having been introduced in 1915 (high-explosive bursting charge, 4 lbs.).

(d.) The re-introduction of a shrapnel for the light field howitzer.

(e.) The introduction of an 8th charge for the light field howitzer, increasing the maximum range from 6,890 to 7,655 yards.

(f.) The introduction of delay action percussion fuzes for use with field gun high-explosive shell. Shell fitted with these fuzes are intended for the destruction of trenches, observation posts, dug-outs, houses, bridges, &c., and for "ricochet fire" against living targets in the open or behind low cover.

(g.) The introduction of a gas shell for the field gun.

The result of the above changes is that both the field gun and the light field howitzer will in future be equipped with four types of projectiles, viz.:—

An ordinary high-explosive shell,
A more powerful long shell,
A shrapnel,
A gas shell,

in place of the previous seven types for the gun and five for the howitzer.

4. Expenditure of ammunition.—As regards the actual expenditure by the Germans during the first period of the Somme offensive, General v. Stein (Commanding "A" Group, First German Army) reports his expenditure to have been as follows:—

(a.) *Average daily expenditure during the artillery duel from the 24th to 30th June, 1916.*

	Rounds.
Field gun battery	1,500
Light field howitzer battery	1,050
Heavy field howitzer battery	520
21-cm. mortar battery (two mortars) ..	200

(*b.*) *Average expenditure on the 1st July*, 1916, *the day of the infantry attack.*

	Rounds.
Field gun battery	2,270
Light field howitzer battery	1,800
Heavy field howitzer battery	940
21-cm. mortar battery (two mortars) ..	400

(*c.*) *Specially high expenditure by individual batteries on individual days.*

		Rounds.
Field gun battery..	over	4,500
Light field howitzer battery ..	„	3,000
Heavy field howitzer battery ..	„	1,200
21-cm. mortar battery (two mortars)	„	500

5. **Supply of ammunition.**—The amount of ammunition which the Germans consider necessary to maintain in the battery positions has gradually increased since the fighting in the autumn of 1915. At the end of 1915, and before the Somme battle began, they considered that the following "iron ration" with the battery was sufficient:—

	Rounds.
Field gun battery	2,000
Light field howitzer battery	1,500
10-cm. gun battery	1,500
Heavy field howitzer battery ..	800 to 1,000
21-cm. mortar battery (two mortars) ..	200

In ordinary circumstances, stocks of 1,000 to 1,500 rounds were considered to suffice for field batteries, but as soon as signs of a hostile attack were recognised, the amounts were to be immediately made up to those given above, and maintained at that level throughout the period of the enemy's artillery preparation.

After the July fighting on the Somme, General Sixt v. Armin (Commanding "B" Group, First German Army) reported that he considered the following quantities of ammunition to be necessary :—

Battery.	In the battery position.	In reserve with the Division.	In reserve with the Corps.
	Rounds.	Rounds.	Rounds.
Field gun	2,200	500	2,200
Light field howitzer	2,200	500	2,200
10-cm. gun	1,600	400	1,600
Heavy field howitzer	1,400	300	1,400
21-cm. mortar (2 mortars)	300	80	300

Finally, General v. Stein (Commanding " A " Group, First German Army) reported in September, 1916, that he considered it essential that the following amounts should be maintained in the battery positions :—

	Rounds.
Field gun battery	3,000 to 3,500
Light field howitzer battery	3,000
10-cm. gun battery	—
Heavy field howitzer battery	1,500 and 300 T gas shell.
21-cm. mortar battery (two mortars) ..	500

It will be noticed that these amounts are almost double those which were considered adequate early in 1916.

Batteries to which ammunition could be brought up by day could manage with a smaller "iron ration," but General v. Stein considered it essential that the whole of the Divisional ammunition columns should be kept filled, the Corps reserve being regulated according to the facilities for bringing up supplies from the Army to the Corps.

6. **Deterioration of German guns.**—From captured documents it is apparent that the rate of wastage of German guns increased very considerably during the past summer, in spite of the repeated instructions on the subject issued by Armies and by the Chief of the General Staff.

This was especially the case with field guns and light field howitzers. In August, the Commander of the First German Army stated that "should such a high rate of expenditure continue, the possibility of replacing these guns is already very questionable. The War Ministry has reported that it is no longer possible to increase the supply."

On the 24th August, the Chief of the General Staff, in a circular letter on the subject, stated that "the wastage of guns in the past few months has been *considerably* in excess of the production."

Much of this deterioration was apparently due to bursts in the bore, caused by "the large number of rounds which are fired in rapid succession and overheat the bore." Other causes were the heating of the ammunition by the sun during the hot weather and inattention to the rules laid down for the care of guns and ammunition. The Germans lay much stress on the necessity for keeping one gun at a time out of action in order to cool and clean it, even during barrage fire.

B.—TRENCH MORTARS.

1. **Trench mortars in common use.**—The German trench mortars* which are most frequently employed are :—

—	Calibre.	Weight of H.E. projectile.	Range.
	inches.	lbs.	yards.
25-cm. heavy *Minenwerfer*	9·84	139 210	262—919 164—514
17-cm. medium *Minenwerfer*	6 69	100	116—1,006
7·5-cm. light *Minenwerfer*	2·95	10	175—1,148
9·2-cm. *Lanz Minenwerfer* (smooth bore)	3·58	8·7	137—492
24-cm. heavy *Ladungswerfer*	9·45	44† 66† 88†	38—290 27—208 22—175
Granatenwerfer (or "stick" bomb thrower).	...	4	66—208

The first three are the regulation rifled trench mortars which form the armament of the *Minenwerfer* companies (*see* page 72).

All these trench mortars fire H.E. projectiles, and the medium, light and Lanz *Minenwerfer* employ gas shell as well.

2. **Flash reducers and fuze caps.**—Among the latest developments as regards these weapons is the employment of flash reducers in connection with the heavy and medium *Minenwerfer*. These flash reducers are similar to those used with howitzers.

As an additional precaution, a thin perforated cap is now screwed on over the fuze to prevent the sparks from the fuze being seen when firing at night.

3. **Increased angle of traverse.**—Hitherto, the angle of traverse of heavy and medium *Minenwerfer* has been 40 degrees, and that of the light pattern 20 degrees. It is proposed to provide a traversing plate or, possibly, a circular platform for these weapons, which will give them an arc of fire of nearly 360 degrees.

---

* Details of the ammunition and employment of the three first named are contained in "Notes on German Shells" (S.S. 420), and particulars of other types of trench mortar are contained in "Particulars of German Weapons for the Close Combat" (S S. 489).

† These are the thin-walled projectiles usually known as "rum jars." Similar projectiles, cylindrical in shape and known as "oil cans," are fired from various types of extemporised mortars. The penetrative power of all these projectiles is practically nil, but owing to the size of the charge their moral effect is great.

C

4. **Pneumatic trench mortars.**—The following particulars of two patterns of pneumatic trench mortar are taken from a document issued by the Chief of the General Staff in January, 1916:—

—	Weight of H.E. projectile.	Weight of H.E. bursting charge.	Range.
	lbs.	lbs.	yards.
15-cm. *Pressluft-Minenwerfer* ...	143	44	110—492
10-cm. *Pressluft-Minenwerfer* ...	13	3	110—547

The rate of fire of both these trench mortars is stated to be one round per minute.

C.—MACHINE GUNS AND AUTOMATIC RIFLES.

1. **The German machine gun** (known as M.G. 08) is of the Maxim pattern and is of the same calibre as the rifle, viz., ·311-inch (7·9-mm.).

2. **Methods of mounting.**—Several new types of mounting for machine guns have been tried; these include a single hinged support, and a low tripod, the legs of which are 12 inches long, with a pivot arrangement which enables the gun to be fired in all directions.

3. **Shield.**—Machine guns have been captured which are fitted with a very small shield; this affords some protection to the head of the machine gunner.

4. **Flash reducer.**—German machine guns are sometimes provided with a muzzle attachment for reducing the flash.

5. **Automatic rifles.**—Three patterns of automatic rifles are at present in use; these are the *Parabellum*, the *Madsen* and the *Bergmann*.

Of these the Parabellum is chiefly used in aeroplanes, the Madsen is the weapon of the "*Musketen* Battalions," and the Bergmann that of the "Light Machine Gun Sections," though it is also used in aeroplanes.

D.—RIFLE.

1. **The '98 pattern rifle.**—The rifle with which practically the whole of the infantry is armed is the '98 pattern Mauser, calibre ·311 inch (7·9 mm.); other older pattern rifles of the same or larger calibres are occasionally met.

2. **Ammunition.**—The ordinary ammunition contains a tapered lead bullet, which has an envelope of steel coated with cupro-nickel; the cap of the brass cartridge-case is edged with *black* lacquer.

In addition to the ordinary ammunition, a certain amount of "*armour-piercing*" *ammunition* is issued in which the bullets contain a pointed steel core. Externally, this ammunition is almost exactly similar to the ordinary ammunition, the only distinguishing marks being a *red* lacquer edging round the cap of the cartridge, and the letter "K" on the base instead of "S." The actual bullet is, however, considerably longer, though the portion projecting beyond the cartridge is the same length. This "K" ammunition is used against aircraft, loophole plates, &c.

An *explosive bullet* now employed by the Germans is similar in appearance to the old-fashioned round-nosed bullet, except that it is longer and the nose is pierced by a small hole to act as a gas escape.

The explosion is caused by an igniting device actuated by the shock of discharge, and takes place in less than one second after firing, independent of impact.

This bullet, which is not a tracer bullet, has been found in the belts of captured German machine guns. Prisoners state that it is intended for use against aircraft, and that normally every 20th cartridge in the belt contains an explosive bullet.

3. **Extra detachable magazine.**—A certain number of detachable magazines (*Ansteckmagazine*) holding 25 cartridges have been issued with the object of providing an increased volume of fire. Rifles fitted with these magazines are awkward to handle, and are only suited for certain phases of trench warfare.

4. **Special sights.**—The ordinary '98 pattern rifle is sometimes fitted with telescopic sights for use by snipers. Various patterns of periscopic sights have also been tried.

E.—RIFLE GRENADES.

An official German text-book, dated 7th August, 1916, states that no more rifle grenades will be manufactured, as it is difficult to obtain any real effect with them owing to their want of accuracy.

F.—HAND GRENADES.

1. **Types in common use.**—The use of the "Cylindrical grenade with handle" (*Stielhandgranate*, sometimes known as the "Jam-pot and stick grenade"), "Ball hand grenade (*Kugelhandgranate*), both of the time variety, and the "Disc percussion grenade" (*Diskushandgranate*), has been continued. A new hand grenade, the "Egg" (*Eierhandgranate*), has made its appearance and is used in considerable quantities. This is a small time grenade of the shape, and about the size of a hen's egg. It weighs only 11 oz. and can be thrown about 50 yards; but its effect, as it is only filled with powder and fired without a detonator, is very small.

C 2

2. Developments.—The Germans do not seem satisfied with their disc percussion grenade, which is in fact somewhat dangerous to handle and very dangerous to pick up if blind. Attempts are being made to convert the time cylindrical grenade with handle to a percussion pattern. Two varieties of such grenades are known : the first, called the *Wilhelm* or the *Friedrich* grenade, relies on the ordinary ball and spring device, which is contained in the upper part of the handle, to retain the striker; the second has a safety bolt, between the striker and detonator cap, which is kept in position by a spring lever on the side of the handle until this is released by the thrower. Blinds of both types are dangerous to pick up.

All these hand grenades, except the last one, are described and illustrated in the pamphlet, "The Training and Employment of Bombers" (S.S. 126, edition of September, 1916). A description of the lever percussion grenade is given in Ia/23752, dated 30th November, 1916.

3. Gas grenades.—Various types have been tried, the earlier grenades consisting of a glass sphere containing a corrosive liquid or producing a lachrymatory or asphyxiating gas. The pattern now in use consists of a spherical grenade about 4 inches in diameter, made of thin sheet iron and containing a lachrymatory liquid, which is scattered by the explosion of a small black powder charge. These gas grenades, however, have never been employed to any great extent.

G.—STEEL HELMETS.

1. Description.—The German steel helmet is made of hard, magnetic, nickel steel, and is rather heavier than our own, weighing complete about 2 lbs. 8 oz. The helmet has a large lug projecting from either side to which a thick, bullet-proof, protective shield can be attached. This shield is very heavy, and is probably intended only for use by snipers and sentries.

2. Value.—The Germans have a high opinion of the value of the steel helmet, "which gained a great reputation among the troops in a very short time. It is considered desirable to equip artillery observers and anti-aircraft posts with steel helmets." As late as the 23rd September these helmets had not been issued universally, as a captured order stated that until the infantry had been supplied no demands from other units could be considered.

H.—"FLAMMENWERFER."

1. Types.—There are three types of *Flammenwerfer* (flame projectors) at present in use:—

> **(a.)** Large *Flammenwerfer*, which are built in at about 27 yards from the enemy's trench. They can cover a front of 55 yards with

flames, the range of the jet being 33–44 yards, and the duration of the flame attack being about 1 minute.

(b.) Small *Flammenwerfer*, which are easily carried on a man's back; the range of the jet is 16–19 yards.

(c.) New type of small portable *Flammenwerfer*, which is 3 to 4 feet long, made of iron and provided with two handles. It is filled with an inflammable liquid and is intended to be carried up to the entrance of a dug-out, &c., lighted and thrown in.

2. **Troops equipped.**—At the beginning of 1916, the 3rd Guard Pioneer Battalion* (6 companies) was equipped with *Flammenwerfer* and had been trained in their use. Each company is equipped with 20–22 large and 18 small *Flammenwerfer*, and is able to cover a front of 1,100–1,640 yards.

3. **Methods of dealing with a flame attack.**—The Germans lay down that the large built-in *Flammenwerfer* must be destroyed as soon as possible by concentrated artillery fire, and that an endeavour should be made to shoot the men carrying the small apparatus, which will then constitute a danger to the enemy's own troops.

I.—LISTENING SETS (called by the enemy " *Moritz.*").

1. **Use by enemy.**—The enemy has derived much information by overhearing messages sent on our telephone lines. Captured documents show that, whereas in November, 1915, practically no identifications had been made by this means, by the 5th March, 1916, the identifications from this source alone equalled the total obtained by all other means.

There is no doubt that the system has been improved and extended since the latter date. Copies of our orders were found in a "listening set" dug-out in La Boisselle at the beginning of July, and it is known that as recently as August information of intended operations was being obtained from this source by the enemy in the Loos salient.

2. **Enemy's precautions.**—The Germans have adopted elaborate precautions to prevent leakage over their own wires, amongst which the principal are:—

(a.) Prohibition of any but the most urgent messages from or to the front line by telephone, and an extended use of visual signals.

(b.) Replacement of the telephone in forward trench systems by speaking tubes.

(c.) Careful maintenance and insulation of telephone circuits.

(d.) Use of codes to conceal the important portions of messages.

---

* The 4th Guard Pioneer Battalion is probably also equipped with *Flammenwerfer*, but the number of companies is not known.

8. Enemy's methods.—Speech is more difficult to overhear than are buzzer signals.

The radius of action of a listening set depends on various factors, but under favourable conditions there is every reason to believe that the Germans can read buzzer signals up to a distance of at least 3,000 yards from the listening set earths. The enemy endeavours to get these latter as far forward as possible by utilizing mine shafts, connecting wires to our entanglements or to earths close under our parapet, &c.

When evacuating positions, it is believed that he makes arrangements to utilize the abandoned telephone connections as earths. All old wires must, therefore, be cut, a considerable length removed, and the ends placed clear of the earth and, if possible, insulated.

V.—GAS WARFARE.

A.—OFFENSIVE.

1. **Cloud gas.**—For making cloud gas attacks the enemy uses cylinders of compressed gas, weighing about 90 lbs. when full, and containing about 45 lbs. of gas compressed to a liquid. The cylinders are built in at the bottom of the trench underneath the parapet; when a discharge is to be made, each cylinder is fitted with a lead pipe which is bent over the top of the parapet. In recent attacks, the enemy has used gas composed of a mixture of chlorine and phosgene, and cylinders have been installed at the rate of two per yard of front.

In recent gas attacks, the Germans have used gas clouds of very high concentrations. This has been attained by employing as many cylinders as possible on a restricted front and by reducing the time of discharge. The duration of an attack may now be as short as 10–15 minutes, although in earlier operations the emissions lasted for hours.

Gas attacks are generally made at night, and several clouds may be sent over at intervals varying from a few minutes up to several hours.

2. **Gas shell.**—The Germans use two types of gas shell, viz., *lachrymatory*, which primarily attack the eyes (tear-shell), and *asphyxiating*, which chiefly attack the lungs (poison-shell), though some of the latter also affect the eyes.

These are principally fired from the 15-cm. heavy field howitzer, the 10·5-cm. light field howitzer, the 10-cm. gun, and the 7·7-cm. field gun. as well as from light and medium *Minenwerfer.*

The lachrymator hangs about for many hours, and is used chiefly for barrage purposes and counter-battery work.

Asphyxiating shell are used either against positions which it is hoped to occupy immediately, or solely for the purpose of causing casualties.

Documents have been captured showing the methods to be adopted in using gas shell, and explaining the need for employing them in very large quantities if they are to have any effect. The Germans lay down that gas shell should be used on a calm day, and that damp weather, but not heavy rain, favours their employment. The temperature, too, affects their use, and they are not likely to be employed if it is below freezing-point.

3. **Gas grenades.**—The various types of gas grenade employed by the enemy are referred to on page 36; they are chiefly used against dug-outs.

4. **Protection afforded by British helmets, &c.**—The British Box Respirator and the P.H. Helmet afford complete protection against al

the enemy's poison gases. The box respirator also gives complete protection against lachrymators, but, in very high concentrations, the P.H. helmet may allow enough lachrymator through to make the eyes water.

5. **Organization.**—Gas operations are undertaken by the 35th and 36th Pioneer Regiments, each of which is composed of two battalions of three companies and a park company. Each regiment has 78 officers, including chemists, meteorologists and other specialists. Two pioneers are detailed to each battery of 20 cylinders.

B.—DEFENSIVE.

1. **Individual protection.**—Each German soldier is supplied with a respirator which consists of an impermeable face-piece, into which is screwed a drum (*Einsatz*) packed with chemicals. The apparatus is carried in a tin box and each man is supplied with a spare drum. The drum has three layers of chemicals and the most recent type is termed the "*Leichtatmer*," to distinguish it from the previous 3-layer drum which was more difficult to breathe through. The windows of the mask are made of a celluloid type of material, which does not dim readily when breathed upon. The masks are made in three sizes.

Great stress is laid upon the correct fitting of masks, and the fit of each man's respirator is tested in a chamber containing lachrymatory gas. This test is supposed to be repeated once a month.

An oxygen breathing apparatus (*Selbstretter*) is also used throughout the German Army, but though available as an anti-gas device, it is more of a rescue apparatus and is chiefly used in mine work.

2. **Collective protection.**—No special design for protecting shelters against gas is laid down in the German Army. The use of doors, curtains, &c., is frequently recommended, but very little has actually been done in carrying out the suggestions.

For clearing gas from dug-outs, ventilation by fires is chiefly relied on. The use of sprayers has been abandoned, and no special type of anti-gas fan has been adopted. On the other hand, cartridges containing chemicals are supplied for clearing gas from dug-outs in obstinate cases. The cartridges are fired from an illuminating pistol, but they do not appear to be altogether satisfactory and are not supplied in large quantities.

Lachrymatory substances in the neighbourhood of shell holes are destroyed by spraying with pyridine. This substance has a very offensive smell and only small quantities are available. It is not very effective.

Very special attention is paid by the Germans to the protection against gas of all arms, artillery ammunition, telephone instruments, &c. Emphasis is laid on the need for keeping them well covered, coating all bright parts with oil, and cleaning and re-oiling after an attack. Artillery ammunition which has been exposed to gas is expended as soon as possible after cleaning.

3. **Alarm arrangements.**—" Gas Alarm " is given in the trenches by means of gongs, bells, sirens, &c. No special long-distance sound signal device appears to have been adopted. Coloured lights are much used for spreading the alarm to the rear.

In the area behind the lines, the ringing of church bells appears to be the chief alarm arrangement.

4. **Organization.**—A special anti-gas officer is attached to each Army Corps, Division and regimental headquarters. Each battalion and company details an officer to deal with matters of gas defence; medical officers are no longer used for this purpose. Anti-gas officers are trained at gas defence courses either behind the lines or in Germany.

Wind observations are made at forward stations on each battalion front and communicated to the Field Meteorological Station at Army Headquarters, which, in turn, communicates every evening with Corps and Divisional headquarters stating the possibility or otherwise of a gas attack. Local wind observations are supposed to be made all along the front by the troops themselves for the guidance of unit commanders.

C.—CASUALTIES CAUSED BY OUR GAS.

Documents and prisoners' statements show that the enemy has suffered very severely from our gas attacks. Thus, in one case, a regiment lost nearly half the effectives of the two battalions in front line and, in another, about 150 casualties were caused in a battalion the strength of which was 440. Cloud attacks have been effective to a depth of at least 5,000 yards. At this distance, 60 men were killed in one company through not having their masks with them. Gas from large trench mortar bombs has caused particularly heavy local casualties and is much feared.

VI.—TACTICS.

A.—OFFENSIVE.

1. General preparations for the attack.—Captured documents show the following to be the principal points which, the Germans consider, demand the careful consideration of a commander before undertaking an offensive operation:—

(i.) An exact determination of the objective.

(ii.) A minute reconnaissance of the enemy's position by every available means (patrols, ground and air observation).

(iii.) An estimate of the infantry force necessary to achieve the object in view.

(iv.) An estimate of the necessary allotment of artillery ammunition, based on the duration of the bombardment.

(v.) The distribution of targets to the artillery.

(vi.) The preparation of a point of departure for the infantry.

(vii.) The zones of attack and the objectives must be clearly defined (every officer, non-commissioned officer and man should know exactly what his task is).

(viii.) Detailed arrangements for the distribution of the infantry in depth.

2. The objective.— "The objective of each infantry formation must be limited in both width and depth. As a rule, the task will be to capture a portion of the enemy's front system, *i.e.*, three trenches situated one behind the other.

"Occasionally, it may be necessary to capture important natural features at some distance behind the front system, in order to secure points for artillery observation.

"It is out of the question to go on and attack the enemy's next position without any pause. For this, a *fresh* and most careful preparation is necessary.

"The objective must be reached at all costs. The tendency to establish oneself in the first trench captured must be resisted, for this is not the main feature of the enemy's defence.

"It is possible that the conditions in the enemy's lines may be such that a continuation of the attack beyond the prescribed line is feasible. It must be borne in mind, however, that artillery support for this cannot be available for some little time. *The decision of a subordinate commander to advance beyond the prescribed objective* is a very momentous one, and must be exceptional."

The above extract from a captured document shows the general principles laid down. These principles were followed by the Germans in their last big offensive (at Verdun), and there is no reason to suppose that they do not still hold good.

3. **The artillery preparation.**—Captured German documents show the following to be the principal objects of the artillery preparation :—

> (i.) To inflict as many casualties as possible.
>
> (ii.) To destroy the enemy's obstacles and trenches, especially his front line.
>
> (iii.) To destroy or silence the enemy's artillery, trench mortars and machine guns.
>
> (iv.) To keep under fire and "muzzle" the enemy's neighbouring trenches during an attack.
>
> (v.) To shell the approaches by which hostile reserves and supplies come up.

The zone covered by the bombardment is always extended beyond the limits of the zone of attack, in order to prevent the enemy from switching batteries from sectors which are not threatened on to those which are being intensely bombarded.

During the bombardment, close liaison is maintained between infantry commanders in the front line and the artillery observers. The German infantry itself is held to blame if parts of the enemy's position are not sufficiently effectively bombarded.

4. **The assembly.**—The Germans do not advocate the construction of special assembly trenches, as they consider that these only attract attention and do not usually give effective protection against artillery fire.

The preparation of additional dug-outs in the first and second line trenches is, however, recommended. These are considered necessary, as a postponement of the attack is always possible and the troops may be exposed to hostile artillery fire for several days.

5. **The approach march.**—Before bringing up troops into the zone of the enemy's artillery fire, German commanders are directed to make a personal reconnaissance, not only of the ground itself, but of the distribution of the enemy's artillery fire over the ground to be crossed.

It is not considered advisable to make use of depressions and sunken roads which are invisible to the enemy, as these are usually under a heavy barrage.

Villages which lie in the enemy's zone of fire are avoided on principle.

6. **The moment for the assault.**—German instructions in this matter are very definite. Surprise is considered essential to success, as it cannot be expected that all the enemy's machine guns will be put out of action by the artillery bombardment.

The assaulting waves, therefore, start the moment the artillery fire is lifted or even before, and follow close behind the artillery barrage. The

Germans consider it better to suffer a few casualties from their own artillery than to give the enemy time to get his machine guns out of their shelters.

It is held that the ideal moment for the infantry to reach the enemy's trenches is before the dust and smoke caused by the artillery fire have cleared away.

7. **The assault.**—The method of assault usually employed by the Germans is a succession of infantry waves in fairly open formation.

The assaulting troops are allotted the three distinct tasks of " clearing," " blocking," and " consolidating."

These tasks may be briefly described as follows :—

> *Clearing.*—The destruction of the garrison. The destruction of machine gun emplacements. The clearing of dug-outs.
>
> *Blocking.*—The protection of the flanks and rear of the assaulting waves by bombers posted to block all approaches.
>
> *Consolidating.*—The preparation of the captured position for defence, and the construction of communication trenches up to that position.

The Germans usually attack in three waves. Each of the three waves may comprise both clearing and blocking parties, closely followed by carrying parties with the material necessary for consolidating. An alternative method is for the first wave to be allotted the task of clearing, the second wave that of blocking, and for the third wave to consist of a reinforcing party, either accompanied or closely followed by the carrying parties for consolidating.

8. **Consolidation of a captured position.**—The Germans make every effort to construct cover and prepare a captured position for defence, during the short period that elapses before the opposing artillery opens on their new position.

The steps taken may be summarized as follows :—

(i.) The trenches are reversed or new trenches are dug (it is often considered better to dig new trenches than to attempt to repair old ones).

(ii.) Obstacles (wire entanglements) are put up.

(iii.) Cover is constructed with the material for dug-outs which has been carried up.

(iv.) Barricades are built against portions of the trench which are still in possession of the enemy. These barricades are usually held by bombers and machine guns.

(v.) Machine guns are placed in position.

(vi.) Communication trenches are constructed leading up to the captured position.

9. Attacks in woods.—When attacking in a wood, the Germans usually employ small assaulting columns following a single assaulting wave, in preference to the usual lines of skirmishers.

10. Raids.—The Germans attach, in theory, considerable importance to trench raids, with the object of obtaining identifications, harassing the enemy and lowering his *moral.* Actually, few raids are carried out by the Germans.

The trench raid is regarded as an operation requiring the most careful and detailed preparation.

A captured report on, and the orders for, a raid made on the British trenches in April, 1916, is probably typical of the German methods as regards the execution of raids. The most noticeable features of this document are the minute and detailed instructions given for every phase of the operation and the close co-operation between all arms, which resulted in the complete success of the enterprise.

The operation comprised :—

(i.) *Preliminary artillery registration,* which was spread over several days previous to the raid and during which every effort was made not to attract our attention to the real point of attack.

(ii.) *A feint bombardment,* which was carried out on the day preceding the raid, in order to distract our attention from the registration that was being carried out by new batteries brought up for the operation.

(iii.) *A feint attack,* which was carried out immediately prior to the real attack, with the object of drawing our artillery fire away from the actual raiding point.

The feint attack comprised :—

(*a.*) Conspicuous registration by artillery and trench mortars of the trenches and wire about 800 yards north of the real raiding point.

(*b.*) The explosion of a mine.

(*c.*) An intense bombardment of about a quarter of an hour.

(*d.*) The lifting of the artillery on to our rear trenches.

(*e.*) The exposure of groups of dummy figures in the German trenches, presenting the appearance of assaulting parties leaving their trenches to charge.

(*f.*) Resumption of artillery and trench mortar fire on the original targets.

(iv.) The *Raid* itself was preceded by an intense artillery preparation, during which our trenches were bombarded, principally with gas shell, and the wire entanglements in front of the point of entry destroyed by trench mortar fire.

At 25 minutes after zero time, the artillery lifted and placed a barrage on our rear and neighbouring trenches,* while machine guns opened on our rearward positions and the communication trenches leading to the objective from both sides. At the same time, the raiding party, which consisted of 5 officers and 55 men, divided into 4 patrols, entered our trenches.

At 50 minutes after zero time, the last man of the raiding party returned to the German trenches.

11. "**Flammenwerfer.**"—(i.) *Allotment.*—*Flammenwerfer* detachments are under the direct orders of the Higher Command, and are placed at the disposal of particular formations for a particular purpose. They may be employed either as a complete unit or by sections or squads. and are placed under the orders of the infantry commander responsible for the tactical execution of the operation in view. This commander must allot a general objective to the *Flammenwerfer* detachment, but he should leave the execution of the task to the *Flammenwerfer* commanders.

(ii.) *Method of employment.*—There are two types of *Flammenwerfer*, the large and the small (for details, *see* page 36). The method of their employment differs considerably though their general object is the same, namely, to master isolated hostile defences which continue to resist, thus preventing the infantry from advancing.

They are regarded as offensive weapons only, and their use in the defence is prohibited except in very special circumstances.

Captured documents indicate that the employment of small *Flammenwerfer* had some measure of success during the Verdun fighting, whereas it was generally found difficult to bring large *Flammenwerfer* up into the forward trenches.

The method of employment of both types may be briefly summarized as follows :—

Large Flammenwerfer are heavy and cumbersome, and their employment requires considerable preparation.

They are intended to be built in in trenches or sapheads pushed forward to within 27 yards from the enemy's position.

They are used preparatory to an infantry attack, their object being to destroy or demoralize the hostile garrison.

The flame attack (which only lasts one minute) should be in the nature of a surprise; it is closely followed up by an assault made by a special assaulting party.

Small Flammenwerfer are principally used against concrete machine gun emplacements and, in combination with bombers, for clearing trenches. They are also used against bombing blocks and forward machine gun

---

* This protective barrage, behind and on either side of the short length of trench which is to be raided, has been employed on several occasions.

positions, in cases where the German line has been penetrated and only a portion of a trench is held by the attackers. In these cases, the *Flammenwerfer* squads can usually advance to within a short distance of their objectives without being seen, and can even work their apparatus from behind cover afforded by traverses or angles in the trench.

A method employed by the Germans with some success in the Verdun battle was for *Flammenwerfer* squads to crawl forward to their objective, making every use of shell holes and other cover, and surprise the garrison. Smoke screens have also been used to cover their advance.

In village fighting they have been used for clearing cellars and the upper stories of houses.

12. **Assault detachments.**—The assault detachments are reserved for purely offensive operations of a special and difficult nature. They are only used when their employment offers a better prospect of success than would an ordinary infantry attack.

The following extract from a captured order outlines their employment :—

" *The assault detachments,* supported by picked squads of infantry, will form the first wave of the attack. They must not be used to stiffen the infantry by being distributed amongst the latter. The individual assault detachments will attack definite objectives and have definite tasks allotted."

Assault detachments are sometimes employed for local counter-attacks. On these occasions, the detachment is brought up a few days before the date of the counter-attack, in order to make a thorough reconnaissance of the ground. The detachments are generally employed independently. Their special training makes it difficult to replace casualties, and it is considered that any closer tactical formation would involve undue wastage.

13. **Trench mortars.**— (*a.*) *Employment.*—The Germans consider that, in the attack, rifled *Minenwerfer* (*see* page 33) of all calibres should be employed in large numbers distributed over a wide front. These weapons support the artillery, and are specially useful against targets which are too close to one's own trenches to be shelled by the heavy artillery.

Heavy *Minenwerfer* (9·8-inch) are intended for use against the most important targets which are capable of offering resistance, *e.g.*, parapets, dug-outs, observation posts, trench mortar and machine gun emplacements, &c., and wire.

Medium *Minenwerfer* (6·7-inch) are used against overhead cover and wire, when no heavy *Minenwerfer* are available or when the targets are beyond the range of the latter.

Light *Minenwerfer* (3-inch) are essentially intended for use against living targets, such as the garrisons of trenches and concentration of troops. During the assault they fire on the communication trenches. A certain number are kept ready on the flanks of the attack to engage any machine guns, &c., which may open with flanking fire. Light *Minenwerfer* are considered suitable for delivering barrage fire. "The demoralization of the enemy is best attained by a bombardment of a few hours duration and of the utmost intensity consistent with accurate fire control."

Heavy and medium *Minenwerfer*, it is considered, should be employed for deliberate, well-aimed fire.

The target sectors allotted to *Minenwerfer* should not exceed 110 yards in width, except when using gas shell.

At the moment of the assault, all *Minenwerfer* are ordered to lengthen their range to the maximum.

(*b.*) *Siting.*—Since trench mortars attract fire and involve a considerable amount of traffic, it is considered that they should be sited away from the infantry trenches and be approached by independent communication trenches.

The choice of positions demands considerable care and foresight, and will depend on the targets which are allotted; a detailed study of aeroplane photographs will be of great assistance.

In selecting positions, the possibility of delivering flanking fire should always be aimed at.

All emplacements for heavy and medium *Minenwerfer* should be shell-proof. Light *Minenwerfer* need not not necessarily be placed in shell-proof emplacements, in which case there must be an ample choice of alternative positions.

(*c.*) *Observation and fire control.*—The necessity for good observation is specially emphasized. Observation posts should, if possible, be in the foremost trenches and should be situated in pairs, one being in the line of fire and the other to a flank, the former being the more important. Observation posts should have good command: heavy *Minenwerfer* should be allotted one each, while one post is sufficient for two medium or six light.

Stress is laid on the necessity of multiple telephone lines, lateral communication between observers and central fire control exercised by the *Minenwerfer* commander, whose dug-out should adjoin that of the infantry commander under whose orders he is placed.

Registration should be masked by means of artillery fire delivered at the same time.

(*d.*) *Ammunition expenditure.*—A document issued in January, 1916, states that for the destruction of trenches the expenditure may amount to two medium and one heavy H.E. shell per yard of trench.

The light *Minenwerfer* require a very liberal supply of ammunition in order to fulfil their tasks.

B.—DEFENSIVE.

1. Method of holding the position.—(*a.*) *Distribution of the infantry.*—The experience of the Somme battle has taught the Germans the necessity of holding the first trench* lightly and of distributing the bulk of the garrison of the First Line Position* in support and reserve, as close as possible in rear. The general principle adopted has been a maximum distribution of formations in depth, but the employment of units side by side.

The first trench* is thinly held by a small but reliable garrison, supported by machine guns. This garrison is intended to be strong enough to repulse an attack, assuming that the men reach the parapet in time, but no stronger. The machine guns are disposed so as to provide flanking fire.

The second trench* is garrisoned by the supports or sub-sector (battalion) reserve. A portion of the garrison is detailed to defend the trench itself and, in particular, the entrances to communication trenches. The second portion consists of special bombing parties, which are held in readiness to rush forward to the support of the first trench, if the latter is threatened. The action of these bombing parties should be prompt and vigorous and they should not wait for orders.

The third trench* is usually occupied by the whole or a portion of the Sector (regimental) Reserve.

In the event of an attack, the Sector Reserve is sometimes moved forward into the second trench, to replace the supports which have gone forward to reinforce the first trench.

(*b.*) *The Divisional Reserve* is usually brought up to reserve trenches on the battle-field as soon as the direction of a hostile attack is ascertained. In some captured documents it is recommended that the Second Line Position should be prepared for this purpose, the Division being responsible for the construction of sufficient dug-outs to accommodate the reserves for several days.

The Germans strongly deprecate the quartering of reserves during a battle in villages immediately behind the front. It was found almost impossible to assemble troops quickly when scattered in numerous cellars, dug-outs, &c., in a village which was being heavily shelled.

(*c.*) *Regimental and battalion battle headquarters* are usually in the immediate vicinity of regimental and battalion reserves.

2. Security.—German commanders constantly impress upon their men that their entire system of defence depends on the measures of security adopted by the troops in the line. Such measures entail :—

(*a.*) Good and constant observation.

(*b.*) An efficient system of alarm.

---

* For an explanation of these terms, *see* pages 9 and 10.

D

(*a.*) *Observation.*—In addition to the sentries in the fire trenches, special listening posts are organized in advance of these trenches, to guard against a surprise attack. It is considered necessary for the sentries to remain in these listening posts even during a heavy bombardment. Whenever possible, therefore, the listening posts are made shell-proof.

During a hostile artillery preparation, it is usually only possible for sentries to observe from shell-proof posts; the remaining sentries are instructed to take shelter, either standing or lying down, in the entrance to the nearest dug-out.

(*b.*) *Alarm.*—Every group† commander and individual man is made to realize that the success or failure of the defence depends entirely on the timely manning of the parapet.

The troops are warned that the moment the enemy enters the German trenches he will begin bombing the dug-outs.

Either the group† commanders or the sentries at the entrances to the dug-outs are held responsible for watching for the moment when the enemy's artillery fire lengthens, and for giving the alarm when the enemy's attack is seen or heard.

The Germans consider it advisable for the sentries posted at the entrances to dug-outs to be armed with hand grenades, so as to deny approach to the enemy and to facilitate the task of ejecting him.

The alarm is constantly practised in the form of a regular drill.

3. **Action of the infantry during the enemy's bombardment.**—The action of sentries has been dealt with in the previous paragraphs, the action of the remainder of the infantry in front line is briefly as follows :—

In trenches where there are no deep dug-outs, the garrisons of sectors of trench which are being most heavily shelled either withdraw to a flank or move forward into the open and lie down about 150 yards in front of the position.

Trenches which are thus vacated are kept under observation from a flank or commanding position in rear, and are covered by flanking fire from the garrisons of neighbouring trenches.

It is considered safer to lie down flat in the bottom of a trench or shell hole than to crouch in a " funk-hole " or badly built dug-out.

Troops are warned against all leaving their dug-outs immediately the enemy's artillery fire ceases, as this may be done in order to induce the garrison to man the parapet, whereupon fire is reopened.

4. **Machine guns.**—(*a.*) *Employment.*—" The battle of the Somme has again shown the decisive value of machine guns in defence. If they can be kept in a serviceable condition until the enemy's infantry attacks, and

---

† A group = 8 men under a non-commissioned officer.

are then brought up into the firing position in time, every attack must fail. The greater the efforts the enemy makes in the future to destroy our trenches before his assault by an increased expenditure of ammunition, the greater the extent to which we must rely on the employment of machine guns for repulsing attacks. These should be brought into action unexpectedly and continue the fight when the greater part of the garrison of the front line trenches is out of action, and the enemy's barrage fire renders it difficult to bring up reinforcements."

The above quotation from a captured document gives a brief definition of the principles which govern the employment of machine guns in the German Army. The substitution of machine—power for man—power, whenever possible, has been one of the principal features of German trench tactics. It has resulted in the allotment of machine guns to a regiment being increased from 6 to 18 (3 machine gun companies); in addition to which, a Division has a machine gun marksman detachment of 3 companies (18 guns) as Divisional troops.

Thus, it may be expected that a regimental sector will have at least 18 guns at its disposal, the Divisional machine gun troops being usually employed either as a reserve or for special enterprises.

The object to be fulfilled in the disposition of machine guns in a defensive position is twofold :—

(i.) To repel an attack on the front line trench.
(ii.) To hold up an advance from the front line trench in the event of the attack breaking through.

In either of the above circumstances, the principal factor which governs the problem of siting machine guns is the necessity of protecting the guns and crews from artillery fire, and of being able to bring them into action *in time*.

For further details as to the German practice in the matter of siting machine guns, *see* page 14.

While every care and consideration is paid to the most suitable disposition of the machine guns of a sector, it is a great mistake to imagine that the Germans will bind themselves to any pre-arranged plan of action. On the contrary, they are adepts at the art of bringing their machine guns into action in unexpected places and at unexpected moments. Prompt advantage is taken of the lip of a crater, a natural rise in the ground, or a commanding point in a parapet, from which a machine gun may be brought into action, particularly on a flank, after an attack has commenced. On ground where corn or rough grass gives concealment, machine guns are sometimes pushed boldly forward in advance of the line and concealed in shell holes.

It is noteworthy that in some parts of the front, the Germans have

lately been heightening short portions of their parapet, possibly with a view to using them for machine guns.

The horizontal barrage fire of machine guns is held to give good results on ground where there is no field of view, and at night or in misty weather.

It appears that machine guns are allotted definite barrage zones on which they register.

(*b.*) *Action of machine guns during the enemy's bombardment.*—German instructions regarding the action of machine guns during the enemy's bombardment may be summarized as follows :—

During a heavy bombardment, machine guns and crews must of necessity remain sheltered in dug-outs. Everything, therefore, depends on the gun commander being able to bring his gun into action on the parapet at the right moment and *in time*. To enable him to do so, the following measures are prescribed :—

(*a.*) The exits to the dug-out must be kept clear of débris.

(*b.*) The gun itself must be kept loaded and ready. Both gun and ammunition must be kept clean and free from dust and grit.

(*c.*) A constant look-out must be kept for any change in the enemy's artillery fire.

(*d.*) Not a moment is to be lost in getting the gun out on to the parapet at the first indication of a hostile assault.

(*e.*) Every gun commander is to be taught to realize that the safety of his comrades depends on his skill and initiative.

5. Co-operation between infantry and artillery. — " The essential conditions for successful co-operation between infantry and artillery are reliable communications and constant mutual touch between the commanders of both arms,"

The two principles contained in the above quotation from a captured document are constantly being impressed upon German commanders.

As regards the first principle, the question of communications has been dealt with under " III. Means of Communication " on pages 24 to 28.

As regards the second, the following procedure seems to be adopted :—

(*a.*) The command posts of Artillery Group Commanders and Infantry Sector (regimental) Commanders are either together or as close together as circumstances permit.

(*b.*) Liaison officers for artillery are permanently attached to infantry regiments, and sometimes to battalions. These liaison officers, who are not necessarily trained artillery officers, are in addition to the forward artillery observers in the front line and, normally, the actual observation of fire is not part of their duties,

The liaison officer acts as the intermediary between the Infantry (regimental or battalion) Commander and the Artillery Group Commander. He transmits the wishes and intentions of the Infantry Commander and, in turn, communicates to him the details of all undertakings planned or ordered by the Artillery Group Commander. In addition, he keeps the latter constantly informed regarding the situation in the front line.

(c.) It has been found useful to establish artillery information centres (*Artillerie-Nachrichten-Sammelstellen*) as far forward as possible. Battalions and companies are informed of the positions of these centres so that they may communicate their requirements and observations.

6. **Artillery tactics.**—During the Somme fighting the action of the German artillery has been almost exclusively defensive. It may be considered under two headings :—

> (*a.*) Barrage fire.
> (*b.*) Counter-battery work.

(*a.*) *Barrage fire.*—Although assault detachments have been trained in following up a barrage, the actual employment of barrage fire during the operations has been purely defensive.

The German experience was that a field battery could not maintain an effective barrage over a zone more than 220 yards in width.

Light-pistols formed the normal method of calling for barrage fire, and it was found that the barrage could be established far more rapidly and effectively if there were forward observation officers. Experience was, however, to the effect that the German barrage was relatively slow in opening.

Numerous orders had to be given to prevent the waste of ammunition which resulted from the frequent calls for barrage fire. Thus in August orders were issued that when barrage was called for, rapid fire was to be maintained for 5 minutes, followed by deliberate fire until counter-ordered. In October and November this was changed to 3 minutes' rapid fire followed by 5 minutes' deliberate fire, which then ceased unless the call was repeated.

All field batteries and most of the 15 cm. howitzer batteries take part in the barrage.

(*b.*) *Counter-battery work.*—Special groupings of heavy artillery are usually formed in each Army for the purpose of counter-battery work. These groupings are separate from the field and medium batteries which are placed under the Divisional Artillery Commanders for barrage fire.

The counter-battery groups consist almost entirely of 21 cm. mortars,

15 cm. howitzers and long range 15 cm. guns. They work in conjunction with aeroplane and balloon observation.

7. **Trench mortars.**—The principles already discussed on page 48 as regards siting, observation and fire control apply equally to trench mortars in defence.

As regards their employment in defence, it is considered that they should not be held in reserve for fear of possible losses. "As soon, however, as a hostile attack is imminent, it is advisable to withdraw the *Minenwerfer* from the first trench and place them in prepared positions in the second or third trenches."

As regards the employment of light *Minenwerfer*, the following extracts from a publication issued by the Chief of the General Staff summarize the German view:—

> "Light *Minenwerfer* in particular will be sited in such a manner that by making full use of their range and mobility, all points where the enemy may be expected to concentrate his infantry can be brought under fire, which should be flanking fire whenever possible."
> "The main object will be to place a barrage on the enemy's starting point at the moment when the assaulting troops are being formed up."

One German Division reported in September, 1916, that only the light *Minenwerfer* could be used with advantage in the battle of the Somme; the medium and heavy were mounted in positions in rear, at points where the enemy was liable to break through.

The *Granatenwerfer*, or "stick" bomb thrower, referred to on page 33, is considered a very valuable weapon, and captured documents show that it is intended to organize a *Granatenwerfer* detachment in every infantry regiment, each equipped with 12 *Granatenwerfer*.

8. **Hand grenades.**—(a.) *General.*—The hand grenade (*see* page 35) is regarded by the Germans as an indispensable weapon in trench warfare, both for offensive and defensive use. The importance attached to bombing has been fully justified by the experiences of the Germans in the Somme battle and it is considered essential that every officer, non-commissioned officer and man, not only of the infantry but of the artillery, should be trained.

While emphasizing the great importance of the hand grenade as a weapon for close fighting, the Germans are careful to remind their troops that the rifle is the principal weapon of the infantry.

(b.) *Training.*—Captured instructions for the training and employment of bombers call for no particular comment, except that special stress is laid on the importance of working round the enemy and attacking his flanks with hand grenades should he effect a lodgment in the line of defence.

That there is still room for improvement, however, as regards training in bombing, is shown by a recently captured order issued by von Hindenburg which calls for further efforts in this respect.

The principal object of the training seems to be to give men confidence in the handling of this weapon and to convince them of its great effect when properly used.

Much time is spent in grenade training when troops are out of the line and every battalion is supposed to have its own bombing ground laid out close to its rest billets.

(c.) *Bombing squads.*—It is usual to have a special bombing squad (*Handgranatentrupp*) in each platoon. This squad is composed of a non-commissioned officer and six to eight picked men. Bombing squads are generally employed independently, though company commanders sometimes combine their three squads for some special operation. Men belonging to the bombing squads do not usually carry rifles or bayonets, but are armed with revolvers, trench daggers and either short spades with sharpened edges or knobkerries.

9. **Counter-attacks.**—" When the enemy has succeeded in penetrating portions of our position, the counter-stroke which affords the best chance of success is that which is at once initiated by subordinate commanders on their own responsibility.

" If, for any reason, an immediate counter-attack cannot be carried out on the spot, a counter-attack carefully and methodically prepared down to the last detail can alone succeed."

The above extract from an order issued by a German Army Group Commander on the Somme lays down the principles which the Germans have always followed. The application of these principles may be briefly summarized as follows:—

(a.) *The immediate counter-attack.*—The object of an immediate counter-attack is to prevent the enemy consolidating his newly-won position and, in particular, bringing his machine guns into action.

The counter-attack must be launched immediately, before the enemy's attack is entirely completed.

The decision to counter-attack must, therefore, come from the front line, and can only be made on the initiative of the subordinate commander on the spot.

The forces employed must be ready to hand and can only consist of the reserves at the immediate disposal of the commander.

It is often advisable to move local reserves forward as soon as a hostile attack is anticipated, so as to launch a counter-attack with the least possible delay.

Vigorous counter-attacks delivered by bombing parties from a flank offer the best prospects of success.

(b.) *The methodical counter-attack* involves considerable organization and preparation.

It should only be undertaken by the order of a higher commander and by employing the reserves at his disposal.

A thorough artillery preparation is necessary. An insufficiently prepared counter-attack almost invariably fails through being too hurried.

The execution of a counter-attack of this nature does not materially differ from that of any other form of attack. This is described under "VI.A.—Offensive Tactics."

10. **Ruses and sniping.**—For remarks on snipers' posts and sniping, *see* under "Snipers' posts," on page 15. The following are examples of ruses which have been employed by German troops :—

(a.) *Dummy figures.*—Dummy placed some 60 yards in front of the German trench ; on moving the dummy, it exploded.

Upright dummy in a shell hole ; small electric battery on the dummy, connected with an explosive charge in contact with an unexploded shell. Slightest movement of dummy caused contact to be made and exploded the shell.

Dummy in German uniform, apparently a corpse, placed in No Man's Land. Patrol going out to secure identification, found a strong German patrol near the dummy. In another instance, the dummy was made to move and beckon, as if for assistance.

Dummy moved along German trench to make our men expose themselves when firing at it ; fire at once opened on our men from a machine gun.

Dummies placed in empty trench to give it the appearance of being occupied.

(b.) *Mechanical devices.*—Bomb buried in a listening post, with the handle exposed, giving the appearance of a half-buried pick. Bomb exploded when picked up or could be exploded by a wire running to a German observation post.

Bomb placed in sandbag on the ground ; friction-lighter fastened to the ground ; bomb exploded when sandbag was lifted.

Small flag stuck in the ground with bomb attached to pole. A small rope was connected to the flag ; on pulling this the bomb exploded.

A patrol found a wire attached to a tree 100 yards from our trench. When the wire was touched, machine gun fire was opened on the patrol.

Small flag found in No Man's Land connected by two wires to a shell hole 10 yards away. On the flag being pulled up, an alarm sounded in the shell hole.

(c.) *Camouflage.*—Snipers have been discovered wearing uniforms made of sandbags, merging themselves in the parapet.

Sniper lying at foot of parapet had his head concealed in a bluish-coloured bag.

For purposes of observation, dummy sandbags are incorporated in the parapet.

Dummy periscopes which remain in fixed positions. Real periscopes are raised inside the dummies from time to time as required.

White crosses erected on the parapet and parados have contained periscopes.

(d.) *Miscellaneous.*—On several occasions Germans (in some cases snipers) are known to have donned British uniforms, generally with the object of deceiving our men during night operations. This deception has been heightened by the repetition of English words of command by German officers.

Various attempts have been made to induce men to expose themselves over the parapet. On several occasions remarks of various natures have been shouted across to our lines. On another occasion a light or fire, which emitted clouds of smoke, was seen to break out and run along the front of the enemy's parapet, a large fire being simultaneously lighted in No Man's Land. On all such occasions the employment of the ruse has been closely followed by traversing machine gun fire.

11. **Reliefs.**—Captured documents show the following to be the principal points to which the attention of German commanders has been drawn as regards carrying out reliefs :—

(i.) Too much attention cannot be paid to detail.

(ii.) Battalion commanders and their subordinates should make a careful reconnaissance and get into touch *personally* with the commanders of the outgoing garrison.

(iii.) Accurate sketches of the position, with a full description of its condition and peculiarities, should be handed over by the garrison to the relieving unit.

(iv.) The points of junction should be ascertained with absolute accuracy, for it often happens that troops carrying out a relief under heavy fire fail to find them.

(v.) The simultaneous relief of all the companies of a battalion is to be avoided whenever possible.

(vi.) Divisional Reserves must not all carry out their reliefs on the same night.

(vii.) *In no circumstances may troops, who are being relieved, withdraw until the relief has been completed.*

(viii.) During a heavy bombardment, and when there is a lack of communication trenches, reliefs are best carried out by small parties moving across country.

(ix.) The early hours of the morning have proved to be the best time for effecting a relief.

VII.—AVIATION.

1. Co-operation with artillery.—It was not till early in 1915 that the Germans considered the advantages of a closer liaison between their artillery and flying corps.

At first aeroplanes dropped marked maps in waterproof covers near the battery that was about to engage the target. The aeroplane then signalled results by means of different coloured lights.

This method was not found satisfactory, owing to the difficulty of distinguishing different colours and the limitation of the range of signals.

About March, 1915, wireless from aeroplanes began to be fairly generally used for artillery work. The battery communicated with the aeroplane by signals composed of strips of canvas placed on the ground. As a rule, the air observer, before going up, arranged with the artillery commander regarding the targets to be ranged on.

About the end of 1915 the Germans tried a lamp with a 10,000-candle power beam for signalling from the aeroplane. With this system sketches had to be thrown out in the old-fashioned way. To facilitate these being found, a special appliance was used, to which inflammable matter was attached, which ignited on contact with the earth. In January, 1916, the German General Staff laid down principles for the employment of and the duties of artillery flights.

"The artillery flight is an artillery reconnaissance and observation unit. It should, therefore, always be placed under the orders of an Artillery Commander.

"The continual employment of the same artillery flight in a particular zone will secure that thorough knowledge of the country, and of our own and the enemy's dispositions, which is essential for successful work.

"As a rule, one artillery flight will be employed at first on a Corps front..

"The duties of artillery flights consist of reconnaissance for the artillery, and observation of artillery fire. They should not be used for other purposes."

During 1916 the use of wireless was greatly extended and the closest liaison between the artillery and the flying corps established.

As regards the employment of kite balloons, the Germans did not make use of this method of observation to any great extent until early in 1916, when a large increase in the number of kite balloons was noticed on the Western Front. They are used by the enemy not only for observation but also for photographic work.

2. **Liaison with infantry.**—Even during the battle of the Somme there was a great want of liaison between the flying corps and the infantry. Infantry aeroplanes (*see* "Means of Communication," paragraph F on page 27) were detailed for reporting the exact position of the front line. The infantry, when requested by the aeroplane, were to indicate their position by means of flares or strips of cloth (20 to 40 inches square). In the event of communication breaking down, these aeroplanes were allowed to transmit messages to the rear.

3. **German anti-aircraft measures.**—During the early part of the war the Germans used single guns with varying results against our aircraft. It was not till August, 1915, that they decided on the advantage of using four guns together. These guns were fired so as to enclose the aeroplane in a square formed by the four shells. If the calculations are made relatively accurately, the target is hit when the aeroplane passes the intersection of the diagonals of the square.

During the same month the Germans also established fighting patrols to attack all hostile machines crossing their lines.

Rockets which rose to a height of 6,500 to 7,000 feet were about this time used for ranging purposes. Later, anti-aircraft guns were also mounted on motor cars. About October, 1915, "K" ammunition ("Armour-piercing," *see* page 35) was issued for use against aeroplanes.

It was not till the middle of 1916 that definite information was obtained of the organization of anti-aircraft units into sections, batteries and groups.

About August, 1916, "Alder B." ammunition was issued exclusively for use against kite balloons.

During the early stages of the battle of the Somme, our aviators, flying at a low altitude, frequently fired on reliefs coming up and men actually in the trenches. The Germans at first replied to these tactics by ordering rifle and machine gun fire to be opened on all aeroplanes flying low. This disclosed their positions and was invariably followed by an artillery bombardment of their occupied trenches. Further orders, therefore, forbade this practice.

Before the end of the Somme battle, the Germans greatly increased the number of their aeroplanes, and large fighting squadrons were told off to attack any of our aeroplanes which crossed their lines.

VIII.—SUPPLY AND TRANSPORT.

A.—MOTOR AND HORSED TRANSPORT.

1. Employment.—At the outbreak of hostilities, the German Army was largely dependent on horsed transport. Mechanical transport was regarded as a useful auxiliary.

The rapidity of their advance, and later the length of the battle front, brought home to the Germans the necessity of motor traction.

The increase in the number of mechanical transport units continued till about March, 1915, but later in the year shortage of petrol, and rubber, gradually affected the maintenance of these units.

To counteract the effects of this compulsory reduction of transport, the Germans then established a network of light railways on the Western Front.

2. Types of vehicles.—According to prisoners' statements the following seem to be the types of vehicles now (1916) in use:—

    (i.) *Supply and transport.*—

        (a.) An army pattern G.S. wagon of field-grey colour, with hood and drawn by two (or, if necessary, six) horses.

        (b.) Civilian wagons of all types.

    (ii.) *Ammunition.*—

        (a.) Army limbers of field-grey colour are used for carrying all small-arm ammunition, field gun and howitzer ammunition.

            Small-arm ammunition wagons are drawn by two horses.

            Gun ammunition wagons are drawn by six horses.

        (b.) Heavy gun ammunition is carried in motor lorries and brought up on light railways.

B.—LIGHT RAILWAYS.

1. Employment.—The Germans have made an extensive use of the light railway system in the occupied portions of France and Belgium, and have extended this system near the front by new construction on a large scale.

The material for this new work has been principally obtained by dismantling some of the less important lines in the interior of Belgium, and by reducing the rolling stock on those lines chiefly used for civilian traffic.

2. New construction.—The light railway systems may be divided into three groups:—

    (i.) 1·00 m. and 0·80 m. gauge, of which the former is the more common.

    (ii.) 0·60 m. gauge.

    (iii.) 0·40 m. gauge.

In the first of these groups, new work has consisted in extending the existing lines in operation before the war. The second and third groups have come into existence since the commencement of trench warfare, and are found only in the forward areas.

As far as possible, 0·60 m. gauge has been used in all new work, as this standard lends itself for several reasons to the requirements of field warfare. Metre gauge has, as a general rule, been used in new construction only where lines of that gauge already existed, and where the use of a different standard would cause needless transhipment. The use of 0·40 m. gauge is restricted to the more forward trench tramways where animal traction is a necessity.

The extent to which new construction is carried out varies on different portions of the front, the two chief factors in this connection being:—

    (a.) The proportion of heavy artillery on the front, and the corresponding need for a rapid and efficient supply of ammunition.

    (b.) The proportion of metalled roads in the sector and the condition in which they are maintained.

Thus in the Ypres sector, where, prior to the Somme offensive, there were nearly three times as many heavy guns as on any corresponding sector, and where the roads are few and in bad condition, the light railway system has been far more highly developed than elsewhere.

3. Traction.—The following agencies are employed:—

    (i.) Steam.

    (ii.) Motor (petrol).

    (iii.) Animal.

On the 0·40 m. tramway system animal haulage is used exclusively. The use of electricity has also been reported.

4. Railway construction during active operations.—During the recent operations on the Somme, the German forward railway systems were of necessity in a state of flux. Light lines sprang into being to serve a definite object, and disappeared with equal celerity as soon as they were no longer required.

Railheads were selected as far as possible to fit in with the normal gauge systems. Where it was essential to form a railhead in advance of the existing main line, a normal gauge extension was constructed to the position required. In certain cases, where the existing main line extended beyond the railhead, the metals of the advanced portion were taken up and relaid to narrow gauge.

C.—RATIONS.

1. **Meat ration.**—The daily fresh meat ration has undergone a considerable reduction during the past year, namely, from 350* g. (12¼ oz.) in December, 1915, to 288 g. (10¼ oz.) at the end of June. Further, one meatless day per week was introduced in June, 1916. According to a statement laid before the Reichstag in October, the fresh meat ration at that time had been still further reduced, viz., to 250 g. (8¾ oz.).

The preserved meat ration was reduced during the same period from 200 g. (7 oz.) to 150 g. (5¼ oz.).

The above amounts are issued to the fighting troops, the fresh meat ration of staffs, columns and trains being only 200 g. (7 oz.) at the end of June.

2. **Bread ration.**—The normal daily bread ration for fighting and other troops is still 750 g. (1 lb. 10½ oz.), though this may be increased when the troops are undergoing unusual exertions. This is normal to peace conditions.

3. **Vegetable and grocery rations.**—In October, 1916, the daily vegetable ration consisted of 1,500 g. (3⅓ lb.) of potatoes or 250 g. (8¾ oz.) of beans, peas, &c.

Groceries at this date included:—

Coffee	..	..	..	25 g. (·88 oz.).
or			
Tea	..	..	..	3 g. (·1 oz.).
Sugar	..	..	..	17 g. (·6 oz.) formerly 20 g.
Butter	..	..	..	65 g. (2·3 oz.).

4. **Drink ration.**—The troops are provided with mineral water by the Intendance Department.

Commanders may order a daily issue of:—

·17 pint: brandy, rum or arrack,
·44 pint: wine,
·88 pint: beer,

when the medical officers consider such an issue desirable.

5. **Tobacco ration.**—The daily ration consists of:—

2 cigars and 2 cigarettes, or
1 oz. of pipe tobacco, or
0·9 oz. of plug tobacco, or
0·2 oz. of snuff.

---

* The meat ration for field service was fixed prior to the war at 375 g. (13¼ oz.).

6. **Arrangements for feeding the troops during a battle.**—
Much stress is laid on the necessity for the troops taking several days'
rations up with them into the line. The amounts considered necessary vary,
but the general opinion is that 5 days' rations are the minimum; these need
not necessarily be "iron rations."

In order to provide the troops with warm food, the Germans issued
solidified alcohol with which food could be warmed up, or else took the food
up in "food carriers"† and coffee cans. The latter method is, however,
rarely applicable beyond the support trenches.

In addition to the rations carried by the troops, large ration depôts, each
containing several thousand rations, were formed close behind the positions;
carrying parties brought these rations up into the trenches whenever pauses
in the artillery fire permitted.

D.—WATER SUPPLY.

1. **Normal arrangements.**—Generally speaking, most of the water
in Northern France and Belgium is not fit for drinking purposes unless
sterilized by boiling or other methods.

Soon after trench warfare became an established fact, the Germans
organized local systems of water supply for the men in the trenches. As
much use as possible was made of existing systems, pipe lines being laid
from existing waterworks or branching off from existing mains. In
other cases pipe lines were laid from wells, and pumps were installed;
intermediate reservoirs were built, or vats, &c., in sugar factories were
employed as reservoirs. In some places new wells were sunk. The pipe
lines were led into villages close behind the front or even into the support
trenches.

2. **Water supply during a battle.**—These methods of supply
sufficed until the battle of the Somme, when the pipe lines were soon cut by
the heavy bombardment, and the water had to be carted or carried up to
the trenches.

To meet these new conditions, the Germans established or took over
existing mineral water factories behind the front, and stored large quantities
of mineral water in bottles in and close behind the line.

The men took two filled water-bottles with them into the trenches, or,
in some cases, were issued with special large tin water-bottles.

---

† Some of these "food carriers" are constructed on the principle of the "Thermos
flask," and keep the food warm for several hours.

IX.—GERMAN MAPS.

1. Scales and types used.—The small scale maps used by the Germans are mainly 1/200,000 and 1/300,000 scales. These are of much the same style as our 1/250,000 sheets 1, 2, 4 and 5. An edition of the 1/200,000 is published for aviators, without contours, and with information as to camps, billets, &c., printed in red.

Of medium scales, there is a 1/60,000 reduction of the Belgian 1/40,000, and a direct reproduction on the same scale of the French 1/80,000. Neither of these gives any information that is not on the originals, except that town and village populations are shown on the 1/80,000.

Large scale maps are mostly enlargements from, or copies of French maps. The 1/80,000 has been enlarged to 1/40,000 and 1/25,000. The result is very coarse, and from our own experience we know such an enlargement to be of small value as an artillery map. French Army *Plans Directeurs* have been copied, and sometimes combined with these enlargements.

It would appear that the Germans use the 1/80,000 for general use and the 1/25,000 for artillery. Trench maps on scales of 1/10,000 and 1/5,000 have been captured, but there is no evidence to show which of these is the regular issue.

On the whole, the German large scale maps give little evidence of originality or initiative. On one map captured recently there is evidence of new survey work on their part, but, with this exception, most of their maps which we have seen are copies, and not up to the standard of our own maps or of those of the French.

2. Conventional signs.—As the maps at present used by the enemy are mostly reproductions of French and Belgian maps, the conventional signs found are those normally used on those maps. Some of the more important signs which are peculiar to German maps, and which may be met with, are reproduced in the table of "Conventional signs commonly used on German maps" (*see* Plate IX).

For *trench maps* new signs have been designed, as with us, to meet new requirements. The signs to denote the same object vary largely, however, even in the same Army, and the same sign is occasionally used with different meanings.

It is evident, therefore, that in studying German trench maps, no assumption must be made as to the meaning of signs. The reference should always be consulted and if there is no reference, common sense must be exercised. By careful study of the map the probable meaning of unknown signs can generally be determined. In the table on Plate IX are given some of the signs commonly used on trench maps the meaning of which seems to be generally accepted.

3. **Methods of squaring.**—German squared maps are divided into kilometre squares, like French maps. The distances in metres from the origin of the grid lines forming these squares are usually marked on the margin. The squares are generally identified by giving each horizonal and each vertical row of squares a letter or number :—

Squares are thus identified as 33. A, 6813, &c. Sometimes each square has its identification written, as shown in one case in the diagram.

To locate a position within a square the Germans divide the square into 25 numbered small squares, and each of these is imagined to be sub-divided into four, lettered a, b, c, d. :—

Thus the description 33. A. 3. b locates a point within a square of 100 metres' side.

Batteries are usually identified by either a letter (a, b, c, d not being used) or a number, the numbers allotted being quite independent of the numbers of the squares. Thus a battery may be signalled 34. B. g or 33. A. 157, g or 157 being the identification letter or number.

The methods of lettering or numbering squares and targets have varied from time to time and between Armies. At the present time the system seems to be—

4th Army (sea to R. Douve) ..	Lettered W—E, numbered N—S.
6th Army (R. Douve to 8 miles S. of Arras)	Numbered E—W and N—S.*
1st and 2nd Armies (N. and S. of R. Somme)	Numbered W—E and N—S.

X.—ORGANIZATION.

A.—THE DIVISION.

1. Divisional organization.—During the past year, while the number of Divisions has increased, their size as regards infantry has been reduced. The probable reason for this is that the output of artillery has exceeded the proportion required for the available increase of the infantry. The choice lay between increasing the artillery of the existing Divisions or forming new Divisions with an all round decrease in the number of rifles per Division.

The latter alternative was chosen, and the 3-regiment organization, which was partially introduced in the Spring of 1915, has now become the normal throughout the German Army.

The following may be taken as the normal organization of a German Division:—

DIVISIONAL HEADQUARTERS.

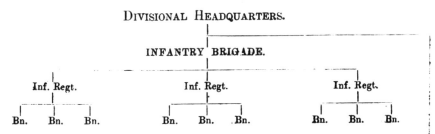

[Each battalion is divided into 4 companies and a machine gun company. Each company (including the machine gun company) is divided into 3 platoons (*Züge*).]

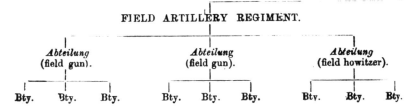

Divisional Mounted Troops—

    1 Squadron.
    1 Cyclist company.

Divisional Engineers—
    3 Field companies.
    1 Bridging train.
    1 Telephone detachment.
    1 Searchlight section.

Divisional Machine Gun Unit—
    1 Machine gun marksman detachment (18 machine guns).

Trench Mortar Unit—
    1 *Minenwerfer* company (16 or 18 trench mortars).

NOTE.—(1.) The Field Artillery of Active Divisions consists of a Field Artillery Brigade of 2 field artillery regiments, each of 6 batteries.

(2.) Batteries have 4 guns or howitzers.

2. Command in the Division.

—The Infantry Brigade Commander is more directly concerned with the *administration* of the three infantry regiments, while the Divisional Commander controls the *tactical co-operation* of the infantry and artillery of the Division.

The Artillery Commander usually commands also the heavy artillery allotted to the Divisional sector.

B.—INFANTRY.

1. Machine guns with infantry.

—An essential change introduced into the German infantry regimental organization has been the increase in the establishment of machine guns. The number of machine guns in a Division has been gradually increased from the normal 24 to the present total of 72 by the addition of extra machine gun units, but for a long time there was no standard establishment, and the allotment varied considerably in the different Divisions.

In September, 1916, the establishment was finally fixed at one machine-gun company (6 guns, 89 officers and other ranks) per battalion, and all the machine gun units have now been reorganized on this basis.

In addition to the battalion machine gun companies, specially trained "Machine Gun Marksman Detachments" (of 18 machine guns) have been formed, and are probably allotted as Divisional troops.

2. Light machine gun sections.

—A number of "Light Machine Gun Sections," some or all of which are armed with the Bergmann automatic rifle, were formed during September and October, 1916, but these are nearly all on the Eastern Front, and none have been engaged in the Somme fighting.

An automatic rifle of the Madsen type, with which two battalions were equipped, has not proved a success, and it is unlikely that more battalions of this nature will be formed; it is, however, probable that sections of automatic riflemen will be attached to companies, as is done in the French Army.

3. **Infantry batteries.**—A certain number of " Infantry Batteries " and " Revolver-gun Batteries" have been identified; these are equipped with 3·7-cm., 5·7-cm. and 7·62-cm. guns, and also with captured Russian and Belgian guns.

These formations appear for the present to be experimental, but will probably in future be allotted permanently to infantry units, *with a view to defence against tanks.*

4. **Assault detachments.**—Another noteworthy feature of infantry organization has been the introduction of "Assault Battalions" (*Sturm-bataillone*) and "Assault Detachments" (*Sturmtrupps*).

These units consist of picked men whose initiative and skill in attack are developed by special training. These units were first used in the Verdun fighting and the idea has since been largely developed.

These units originally formed Army troops; they are now being formed in each Corps and Division, and may eventually form part of the regimental organization.

C.—ARTILLERY.

1. **Higher organization.**—During the past year a radical change in the artillery tactical organization has taken place. The heavy artillery has passed from the control of the Corps or Army to that of the Division.

Before the Somme battle, the field and heavy artillery on each Divisional front had already been amalgamated into mixed groups, sometimes with a Corps or Army heavy artillery reserve for counter-battery work.

Normally, the field and heavy batteries allotted to the sector held by a Division in the line are placed under one artillery commander. The Divisional front is then divided into two, three or four sectors, to each of which is allotted a mixed group of field and heavy batteries. When Divisions are relieved, the heavy artillery remains in position and passes to the incoming Division.

2. **Allotment of batteries to Divisional sectors.**—A normal allotment of batteries to the sector held by a Division on a quiet part of the front would be:—

Field batteries	..	..	..	..	12
Heavy batteries	..	..	..	..	6
Total batteries	..	..	..	..	18

On the battle-fronts at Verdun and on the Somme, however, this allotment has in many instance been doubled, the usual being about :—

Field batteries	..	..	..	..	..	20
Heavy batteries	..	..	..	..	..	10
Total batteries		..	..	..	..	30

3. **Organization of batteries.**—All batteries now have 4 guns, with the exception of heavy gun batteries on railway mountings and heavy howitzers (mortars) of 21-cm. and over, which have only two guns or howitzers apiece.

The 4-gun battery is divided into two sections (*Züge*).

The Field Artillery Regiment and Field Artillery, *Abteilung* are now administrative rather than tactical groupings. Foot Artillery Batteries are now usually independent, and their original regimental organization has been broken up.

D.—CAVALRY.

The Germans have made no use of cavalry in the Somme fighting. Since the beginning of the battle, the only cavalry Division on the Western Front has been transferred to the east.

During the past two months, a number of the reserve cavalry units have been dismounted and converted into infantry.

E.—AVIATION.

1. **Higher organization.**—The whole of the German Aviation and Balloon Service has recently been placed under the sole command of Lieut.-General von Hoeppner.

At each Army Headquarters there is a Staff officer for the Aviation Service who co-ordinates the work of the aeroplane and balloon units.

2. **Aviation units.**—The main feature of the aircraft organization is the sharp distinction which is drawn between the different spheres of aerial activity. Fighting, reconnaissance and artillery work are carried out by separate units, which are numbered in different series.

The fighting machines are organized in 7 " Battleplane Squadrons " (*Kampfflugzeug-Geschwader*), each sub-divided into 6 flights* (*Staffeln*). At first these were kept under the direct orders of General Headquarters, but latterly the flights have been split up and attached to Armies and Corps.

---

* A flight consists of 6 or 7 machines, except in the case of a naval flight (*Marine-Feldflieger-Abteilung*), which has 14 or 15 machines.

The "Reconnaissance Flights" (*Feldflieger-Abteilungen*) are normally allotted at the rate of one per Corps sector. Their normal tasks are photography and bombing.

The "Artillery Flights" (*Artillerie-Flieger-Abteilungen*) are used solely for artillery observation and registration.

3. Organization of the Air Service on the Western Front.—
The following table shows approximately the normal distribution of aviation units on the Western Front :—

Under General Headquarters—
6 Battleplane squadrons = 36 fighting ⎫
   flights (*Kampfstaffel*) .. .. ⎬ = 216 machines.
                                    ⎭
Under each Army Headquarters—
1 Pursuit flight (*Jagdstaffel*) .. .. = 6 machines.
2 or 3 Reconnaissance flights.. .. = 12 or 18 machines.
Under each Corps Headquarters—
1 Reconnaissance flight .. .. = 6 machines.
1 Artillery flight .. .. .. = 6 machines.

This distribution has, however, been greatly modified during the battle owing to the great concentration of aviation units on the Somme.

The following units have actually been identified in the Somme area :—

22 Fighting and pursuit flights .. = 132 machines.
23 Reconnaissance flights .. .. = 138 machines.
15 Artillery flights .. .. .. = 90 machines.
                                    ———
                                    360
                                    ———

F.—ENGINEERS.

1. **Pioneer field companies.**—No important change in the employment of engineers has come to light during the Somme fighting.

The number of pioneer companies (exclusive of mining companies) now formed allow of 3 "Pioneer Field Companies" for every German Division in the field.

2. **Mining companies.**—"Mining Companies" are more or less permanently allotted to sectors of the front. Several have been identified in the Somme area, where they are probably employed on the construction of dug-outs.

3. **Special troops.**—The 35th and 36th Pioneer Regiments provide gas personnel, and the companies of the Guard Reserve Pioneer Regiment are principally employed with *Flammenwerfer.*

4. Infantry pioneer companies.—In addition to the regular field companies and mining companies, a number of infantry regiments have formed their own "Infantry Pioneer Companies" and "Tunnelling Companies." During heavy fighting, these temporary units are usually reabsorbed into their regiments.

G.—TRENCH MORTAR UNITS.

Every German Division now has a "Minenwerfer Company" allotted to it.

The *Minenwerfer* company is divided into three sections as follows :—

Heavy section ..	..	4 Heavy *Minenwerfer* (25-cm.).
Medium section..	..	8 Medium *Minenwerfer* (17-cm.).
Light section ..	..	6 Light *Minenwerfer* (7·5-cm.).

The total strength of a *Minenwerfer* company is 8 officers and 202 other ranks.

H.—SURVEY UNITS.

1. The *Vermessungs-Abteilung* (Survey Section) is an Army unit. It corresponds closely to our Field Survey Company, *i.e.*, it is responsible for trigonometrical and topographical work, the preparation of artillery maps and boards, and the fixing of aiming points, survey posts, &c., for photography (including panoramas), printing (maps and letterpress), and the supply and issue of maps.

2. The *Artillerie-Mess-Trupp* (Artillery Survey Section) is an artillery unit. These sections are normally attached to a Division, but do not move with it. There is probably one per Divisional sector.

The *Artillerie-Mess-Trupp* consists of the headquarters (*Mess-Zentrale or Haupt-Messtelle*) and a number, not exceeding four, of survey posts (*Messtellen*). The posts are occupied with the intersection of gun flashes and of all important targets, and with observation of fire and registration of their own guns.

(NOTE.—The name *Mess-Plan-Abteilung* was formerly used, but it is probable that it was merely an early name for the unit now known as *Artillerie-Mess-Trupp*.)

3. The *Schall-Mess-Trupp* (Sound Ranging Section) is an artillery unit, usually attached to a Divisional sector. It works in close conjunction with the *Artillerie-Mess-Trupp*.

The above organization is extremely like our own. The *Artillerie-Mess-Trupp* and *Schall-Mess-Trupp* are artillery units, and not apparently part of the Army Survey Section, as with us. Information obtained by *Artillerie-Mess-Trupps* is sent first to the troops, and then to the *Vermessungs-Abteilung* for accurate compilation. It is the duty of the *Vermessungs-Abteilung* to print and distribute all information gained from various sources, and this probably includes information about hostile batteries. It seems likely, however, that most of the work done by the compiling officers of our Field Survey Companies is done in the German Army by the *Mess-Zentrale* of the *Artillerie-Mess-Trupp*, though there is no definite information on this point.

The whole of the Survey Department in the German (as in the French) Army is classified as " Artillery " for pay. The prefix Artillerie *does not, therefore, mean that these are artillery units in our sense of the term.*

XI.—HIGHER COMMAND.

The tactical unit, which at the beginning of the war was the Army Corps, has now become the *Division*, which has been reorganized on a more mobile basis than before (*see* page 67). A great number of independent Divisions now exist.

The Corps staffs have been retained, although not always with their original Divisions.

The necessity for the rapid relief of a large number of Divisions in the Somme battle, and the consequent continual change of Corps staffs, soon led to the adoption by the Germans of the system of Group Sectors (similar to our Corps Sectors), each having 3 or 4 Divisions in front line. Thus the 1st Army (North of the Somme) is divided into four Groups: A, B, C, D.

Normally an *Army* consists of 8 to 12 Divisions, though this number is greatly increased during severe fighting as at Verdun and on the Somme, where an Army may have as many as 30 Divisions temporarily under its command.

There are now 10 Armies on the Western Front. A new one (the 1st) was formed in July, owing to the operations on both banks of the Somme becoming too large to be handled by a single Army Command.

Since von Hindenburg was appointed Chief of the General Staff, the system of *Groups of Armies* has been extended to the Western Front. The German forces between the sea and the Moselle are now divided into three main Groups of Armies—under the Duke of Württemberg, the Crown Prince of Bavaria, and the Imperial Crown Prince, respectively.

XII.—GERMAN MAN-POWER.

1. **Army in the Field.**—Germany's effort to raise her man-power to the highest pitch of strength, both in effectives and reserves, culminated early in 1916, when the Verdun battle commenced.

In June, 1916, although the Army in the Field was composed of men of considerable training and, so far as 75 per cent. were concerned, seasoned fighters, there were no reserves of the same quality of man in the depôts in Germany or behind the front.

The losses at Verdun accounted for the balance of the 1915 Class, and caused the great majority of the 1916 Class to be drafted into the line. The 1916 Class had received the most prolonged and careful training given to any recruits since the outbreak of war, so that the incorporation of these 19-year old boys did not mean any weakness in the fighting ability of the troops.

2. **Reserves in depôts.**—In the depôts in Germany in June, 1916, there were :—

        (1.) The remainder of the 1916 Class.
        (2.) Healed wounded from Verdun.
        (3.) The whole of the 1917 Class.
        (4.) Men " combed " from reserved occupations.

3. **The 1916 Class.**—The men of this class were called up for training in the various Army Corps Districts of Germany between March and September, 1915. They were required for drafting purposes from March, 1916, onwards, and by the middle of July, 1916, they were completely incorporated in the field units.

4. **The 1917 Class.**—The earliest of the 1917 Class were recruited in December, 1915, the majority being called up in March, 1916, and by the end of May the whole of this class was in training in every Army Corps District in Germany. These men formed a considerable portion of the drafts sent to the Western Front in October and November, 1916.

5. **The 1918 Class.**—This class has now been called up for training in every Army Corps District in Germany, replacing the 1917 Class in the depôts.

6. **" Combed " men.**—The system of replacing men in reserved occupations by woman labour, Poles, and prisoners of war has been steadily going on since July, 1915. The farmer class was combed out thoroughly in the Autumn of 1915.

In March, 1916, the mines, munition factories, railways and civil service were combed, and a remarkable number of the drafts to the line since September, 1916, consisted of men from these occupations.

7. **Returned wounded.**—The troops holding the line in June, 1916, contained a comparatively high percentage of active soldiers and reservists

(about 20 per cent. of the whole forces on the Somme on the 1st July were of this class), a condition obtained by the return of recovered wounded from the hospitals. The return of wounded men to the front line is becoming more marked as the shortage of suitably trained recruits is felt. Men are now being sent to the front with physical defects which, a year ago, would have secured their discharge from military duty. How much this affects the class of the drafts is shown by prisoners of the 55th Res. Inf. Regt. taken on the 13th November, 1916. Out of 545 examined, 35 per cent. were men returned from hospital.

8. **Permanently unfit.**—In the spring of 1915 Germany, anticipating a shortage of man-power, made arrangements to call up and train men who, previous to the war, had been rejected by the doctors at the annual recruiting musters as being "Permanently unfit for any military service." Men were also called up who, as a result of wounds received during the first six months of the war, had been discharged as unfit for all further duty.

These men were called up, examined, and classified in the following categories:—

> (1.) Fit for active service.
> (2.) Fit for garrison duty.
> (3.) Fit for labour employment.
> (4.) To come up for further examination.

The process of calling up and selecting men for service from this class went on during the last six months of 1915, as many as three and four successive musterings being held in each district.

9. **Conclusions.**—When the battle of the Somme began, the German Army on the Western Front was composed of well-trained and experienced soldiers, and despite all efforts made to maintain the quality of the troops by a special system of selection, by transferring men from garrison units and labour companies to regiments at the front, and by taking partially recovered men from hospitals, it has not been possible to replace the losses on the Somme without drawing very heavily on the practically raw recruits of the 1917 Class.

In sending drafts to the Western Front, men combed from reserved occupations, and called up for training with the 1917 Class, have been selected in preference to employing the youths of that class, although the combed men had had less training.

The battle of the Somme has, therefore, accounted for the 1916 Class, 75 per cent. of the 1917 Class, and a very considerable number of men who, during $2\frac{1}{2}$ years of war, were considered indispensable. This leaves the German Army with reserves of lower quality than ever before, namely, boys born in 1898, and such further "indispensables" as may be obtainable when the scheme of reorganization of the civilian forces is complete.

XIII.—ORGANIZATION OF GERMAN MEDICAL SERVICES.
(With special reference to the arrangements during the Somme Battle.)

1. **General.**—The German medical organization for battle consisted of the following échelons from the firing line to the back areas:—Regimental Medical Service; Bearer Companies (Field Ambulances); Field Hospitals; Motor Ambulance Convoy or Column; War Hospitals; Ambulance Trains and Temporary Ambulance Trains; Advanced Depôts of Medical Stores.

2. **Regimental medical service.**—Normally there are with each battalion 2 medical officers, 4 medical non-commissioned officers (1 with each company). and 16 stretcher bearers; with a senior medical officer for the regiment. At the end of May, 1916, a fifth medical non-commissioned officer was added to each battalion. The stretcher bearers are borne on the establishment as non-combatants and wear the Red Cross brassard.

In the trenches, each company formed a medical dug-out or aid post just behind the fire trench, but owing to the large number of casualties amongst the medical officers, it was considered inadvisable to let the battalion medical officers go forward to the fire trench.

A large regimental aid post or dresing station (*Truppenverbandplatz*) is established further back, usually in or near the second support trench. The accommodation is in well constructed dug-outs or in cellars. A warning was issued against the use of buildings on account of danger from our artillery fire. The dug-outs are constructed to hold 30 wounded. A telephone is provided and supplies of lighting materials, extra rations, dressings and medical comforts to cover periods of 5 days or more are maintained in the aid post.

Similar aid posts are formed for groups of four batteries of artillery, if they are not too far apart.

The personnel on duty in a regimental aid post appears to have been at least 3 battalion medical officers, and a detachment of 8 stretcher bearers with 2 stretchers from the bearer company. Wounded are brought to the regimental aid post by the battalion stretcher bearers, and are kept there as short a time as possible, being evacuated from them by the bearer company.

In back areas the regimental medical service opens a local medical inspection room and ward for detained cases (*Ortskrankenstube*), where patients may be kept up to 5 days.

3. **The Bearer Company** (*Sanitätskompagnie*) or Field Ambulance consists of elements equivalent to the bearer division and the tent division of

our Field Ambulance. There are 208 stretcher bearers in two sections with non-commissioned officers and other ranks under officers who are not medical officers, and with a medical officer in medical charge of the sections ; and there is also a main dressing station detachment of 8 medical officers including the senior medical officer in command.

There are 3 of these companies in each Corps. During the battle of the Somme this was not found sufficient, and there was a demand for 2 bearer companies for a Division in the fighting line. The bearers of the one company became exhausted, and it was necessary to establish a relief company to cope with the work of collecting and bringing back wounded.

The posts established in action by the bearer company were :—

(a.) A wagon rendezvous (*Wagenhalteplatz*).
(b.) A main dressing station (*Hauptverbandplatz*).
(c.) A collecting station for slightly wounded (*Leichtverwundeten-sammelplatz*).

(a.) *The wagon rendezvous* is placed in advance of the main dressing station and about 4,000 yards behind the regimental aid post. Dug-outs are constructed at this post, and arrangements are made for giving hot food and drink to wounded coming back. A dump for the issue of medical and surgical material to the regimental medical service has also to be maintained by the bearer company at or near the wagon rendezvous. The post is provided with a telephone. The personnel consists of a small detachment of the stretcher bearers under a non-commissioned officer, and a medical officer is placed on duty there from time to time by order of the Divisional Assistant Director of Medical Services. One or more of the ambulance wagons of the company are kept constantly at the wagon rendezvous, and go forward at night to meet the bearers bringing back wounded. The wagon rendezvous performs much the same function as our advanced dressing station.

(b.) *The main dressing station* is established in a shell-proof shelter in some village 6 or 7 miles from the front line. The personnel may be reinforced from the regimental medical services or from field hospitals ; but it is not to be used for reinforcing or replacing medical officers of either of these échelons. All wounded coming back from the regimental medical service must pass through this post. Two or more motor ambulance cars are allotted to it, and one motor omnibus.

The walking cases are sent back to the main dressing station, after being collected at the wagon rendezvous, in small groups and in march formation.

Every wounded man must have two diagnosis tallies (field medical cards) attached. These tallies have two red perforated margins. If a man is able to walk, both margins are torn off; if classed as fit for transport, one margin is torn off; if unfit for transport, the card is left intact. A man coming back to the main dressing station or wagon rendezvous without a field medical card, or without authority, is sent back to his unit, unless he is found to be suffering from sickness or wound, in which case the card is attached at the main dressing station and the unit informed. This procedure is adopted to prevent men straggling back from the front who have nothing the matter with them.

Amongst the special equipment attached to one of the main dressing stations in a Corps area is a water sterilizing wagon.

(c.) *The collecting station for slightly wounded* is established further back, at or near an entraining station. The walking cases are sent on from the main dressing station either in march formation, as before, or in the motor omnibus or other vehicles.

The following were the positions of these échelons of the bearer company allotted to the 4th Infantry Division when it held a front line at the Bois des Foureaux :—

WAGON RENDEZVOUS.—Dug-outs on the unmetalled road about $\frac{1}{4}$ mile south of Ligny-Thilloy (1/100,000 map), with dug-outs for refreshment post, and surgical and medical dump somewhat further forward.

MAIN DRESSING STATION.—At Villers-au-Flos.

SLIGHTLY WOUNDED COLLECTING STATION.—At Vélu.

4. Field hospitals, normally 12 per Corps, are under the control of the Corps D.D.M.S. They were used in the same way as we use casualty clearing stations for the retention of cases unfit for transport and for special cases. The number of medical officers in each is six. Normally equipped for 200 beds they are expected to expand to any extent. They are opened in various villages in the back area.

Field hospitals were allotted for the following classes of sick and wounded from the 4th Division Bearer Company when the Division held the Bois des Foureaux :—

Advanced operating centre at Villers-au-Flos (near the main dressing station).

Severely wounded at Barastre.

Dental cases at Ytres.

Special surgical cases at Bertincourt.

Gassed cases at Ruyaulcourt.

Infectious cases at Vélu.

Röntgen ray examination at Vélu.

5. Motor ambulance convoys.—The composition of these has not been definitely ascertained. There was no war establishment laid down for them before the war. They appear to be a collection of motor ambulance cars and omnibuses, parked under an officer at some village or locality in telephonic communication with medical units, and used for the conveyance of sick and wounded from the main dressing station to the entraining station or to field hospitals on demand.

The number of these motor ambulance convoys appears to be one to each Army Group.

There is a note in one document to the effect that it is better to keep the vehicles of a motor ambulance convoy parked together in one locality, rather than to distribute a number to medical units. They are thus available on demand where they are most wanted, and demands are sent direct from the unit concerned to the officer in charge of the column.

6. **War hospitals** (*Kriegslazarette*) are used in much the same way as we use stationary hospitals in advanced areas. The number is not fixed and depends on localities available for opening them. Their equipment and personnel are obtained, as required, to a great extent from local resources or depôts of medical stores; but there is a nucleus of the personnel in the form of a definite unit called the War Hospital Detachment (*Kriegslazarettabteilung*), mobilized in the proportion of one for each Corps. Each detachment has 19 medical officers, a dentist, 3 pharmacists, and subordinate ranks.

They are intended for the more or less continuous treatment of special classes of wounds and injuries, which are not sent back to Germany.

7. **The ambulance convoy detachment** (*Krankentransportabteilung*) is a definite unit, divisible into three sections and allotted in the proportion of one to each Army. Its personnel consists of 7 medical officers with subordinate ranks, and its function is to open reception shelters, dressing stations and refreshment rooms at stations where sick and wounded entrain, and take care of the latter while waiting evacuation by railway. It is also a distributing centre for classifying patients for evacuation to various field hospitals or war hospitals, opened for the reception of special cases in the villages in Army and advanced Lines of Communication areas. It makes arrangements for the comfort of sick and wounded during the journey back, and, with the special equipment held for the purpose in advanced depôts of medical stores, fits out empty returning trains as temporary ambulance trains.

The unit is used for the same purpose as we use the evacuation section of our casualty clearing stations.

In connection with the operations of the 4th Division, noted above, an ambulance convoy detachment was working at Vélu.

8. **Ambulance trains.**—In connection with the operations of the 1st Army during the Somme battle, ambulance trains ran to Epehey and temporary ambulance trains for sitting-up cases to Hermies. Empty return trains also took slightly wounded and sick from Croiselles and Quéant to Cambrai, and, as far as possible, both slightly and severely wounded were sent back on the narrow-gauge railway Bellicourt—Caudry.

9. **Advanced depôts of medical stores.**—These are on the Army Line of Communication. For the 1st Army, during the Somme operations, depôts were opened at Cambrai and Valenciennes, with advanced issuing stores at Epehy and Futy-en-Artois. The Divisional bearer company is responsible, as already noted, for bringing up stores to a dump for issue to regimental medical services.

1.—PORTION OF GERMAN FRONT LINE POSITION. (From Trench Map, front wire omitted.)

SCALE = 1:10,000

Yards 100 50 0   500   1000 Yards

A Saps.   BB Second support trench.   CC Switch.

PLATE II.

—

FIG. 2.

WIRE ENTANGLEMENT.

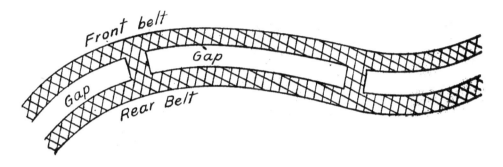

FIG. 3.

CONCRETE OBSERVATION POST.

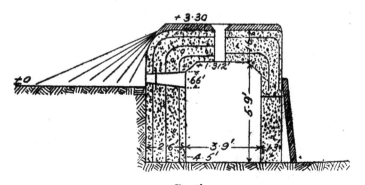

Section

PLATE III.

—

Fig. 4.

Subterranean Observation Post.

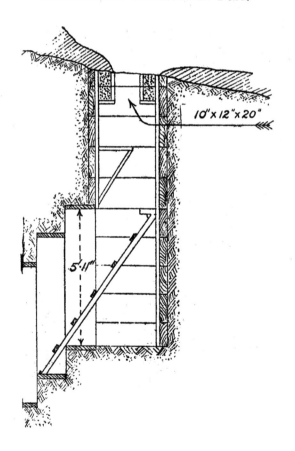

PLATE IV.

—

FIG. 5.

DUG-OUT FOR 5 GROUPS (5 N.C.O.'S AND 40 MEN).

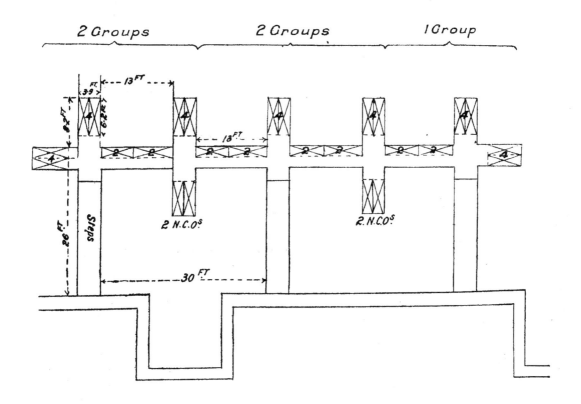

 = Bed for 2 men.

PLATE V.

FIG. 6.

TWO-STOREY DUG-OUT.

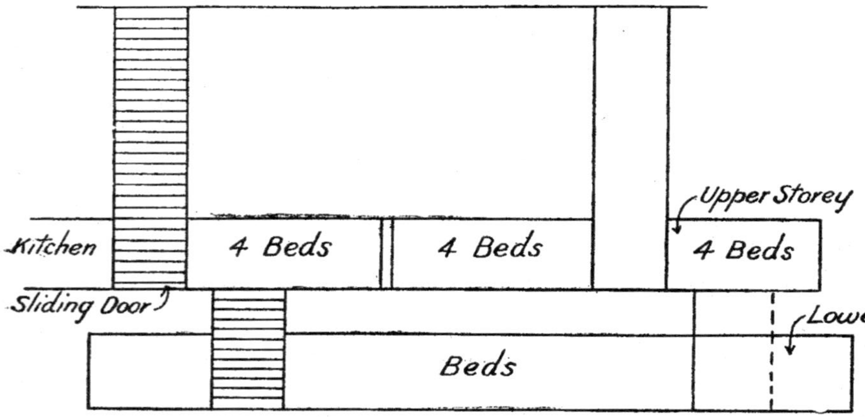

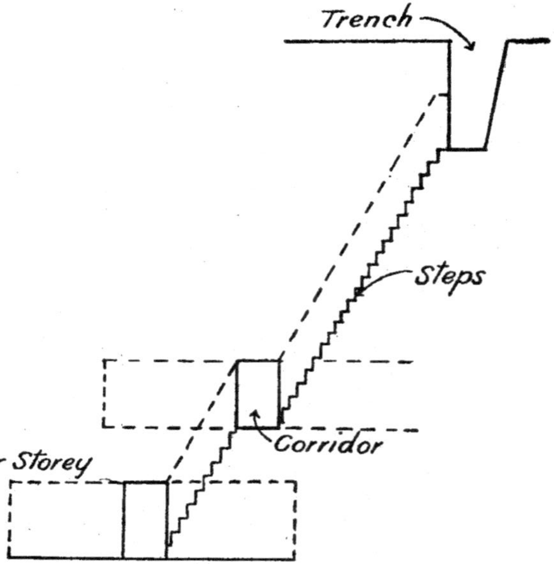

Trench

Steps

Corridor

Cross Section.

Lower Storey

Upper Storey

4 Beds

Lower Storey

4 Beds

4 Beds

Beds

4 Beds

Kitchen

Sliding Door

Longitudinal Section.

PLATE V—*continued.*

FIG. 7.

CONCEALED MACHINE GUN IN FLANK.

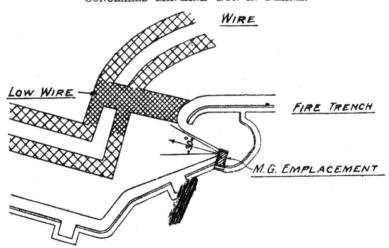

PLATE VI.

Fig. 8.

Sketch Showing Position of German Machine Gun behind Parados.

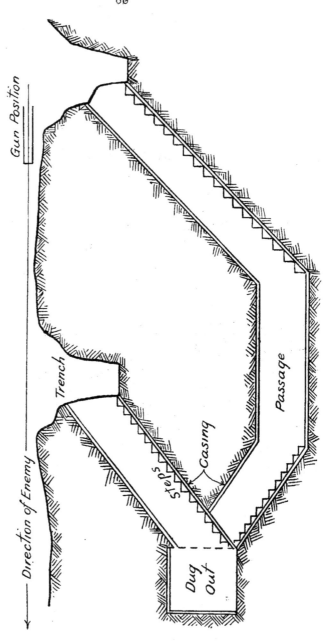

PLATE VI—*continued.*

FIG. 9.

MACHINE GUN EMPLACEMENT.

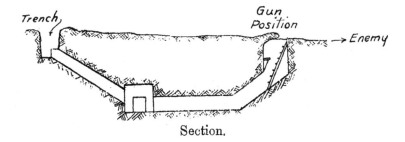

Section.

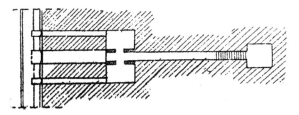

Plan.

Note the three exits from the dug-outs.

PLATE VII.

—

FIG. 10.

REINFORCED CONCRETE SHELTER FOR MACHINE GUN.

Scale : 1 : 50.

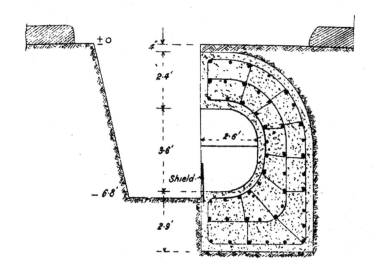

PLATE VII.—*continued.*

FIG. 11.

TRENCH MORTAR EMPLACEMENT.

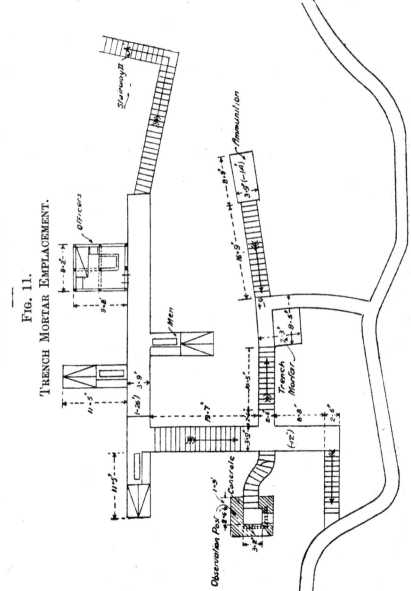

PLATE VIII.

—

FIG. 12.

SKETCH PLAN OF PART OF A BATTERY.

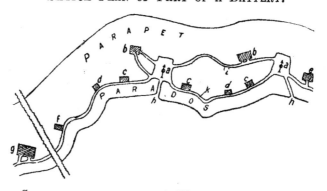

a. Gun.	*f.* Aid post.
b. Men's dug-out.	*g.* Dug-out outside battery.
c. Shell store.	*h.* Embrasure towards reference
d. Cartridge store.	point
e. Orderly and telephone room.	*i.* Front connecting trench.
	k. Rear connecting trench.

PLATE VIII.—*continued.*

FIG. 13.

ARTILLERY OBSERVATION POST.

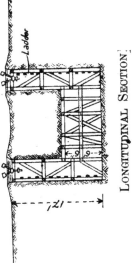

LONGITUDINAL SECTION.

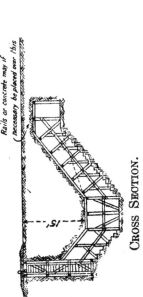

CROSS SECTION.

CONVENTIONAL SIGNS COMMONLY
USED ON GERMAN MAPS.

Fire and communication trenches } (Graben).
prepared for defence.

Ordinary communication trenches (Weg).
The distinction between fire and other trenches is not always made.

Wire entanglement.

Trench railway (Feld-bahn).

Battery fixed by photography.

Heavy Minenwerfer.

Light Minenwerfer.

M.G.   (Occasionally).

Grenade store (or shell magazine).

Screen from view.

Telephone station with cable.

Searchlight.

Pioneer dump.

Dressing station.

Well. (o Br.)

Headquarters. Usually some form of circle with flag. The number of circles increases with the importance of the H.Q. but the signs vary largely.

Coy. Commander. (K.F)

Shaft of mine.

Unsafe ground with mine shafts.

Turnpike. (Ch. Hs.)

PLATE IX

Sch.   **Barn.**

Zgl   **Brick-kiln.**

⊠   **Telegraph detachment.**

Field signalling detachment.

Wireless telegraph station.

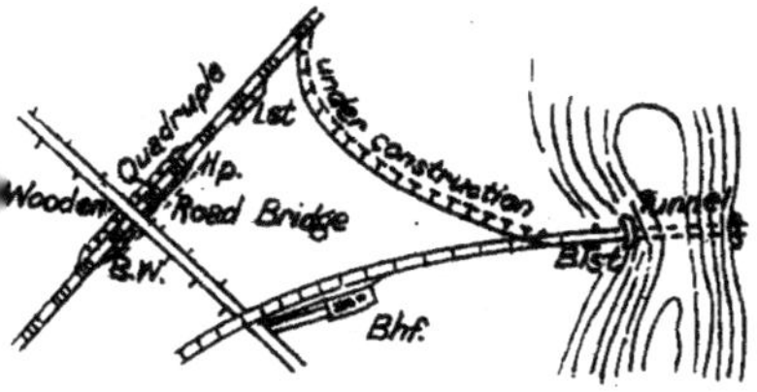

Bhf. **Bahnhof (Station)**.
Hp. **Haltepunkt (Stopping place)**.
Blst. **Blockstation (Block signal station)**.
Lst. **Ladestelle (Loading platform)**.
B.W. **Bahnwärter (Plate-layer's hut)**.

3·7 cm. Revolver Gun.

5 cm. Belgian Gun.

7·7 cm. Field Gun.

Anti-Aircraft Gun.

9 cm. Field Gun.

90 mm. and 95 mm. French Guns.

10·5 cm. Light Field Howitzer.

10 cm. Gun. (newer pattern).

10 cm. Gun (older pattern).

12 cm. Gun.
12 cm. Belgian Gun.
15 cm. "Ringkanone."

13 cm. Gun.

15 cm. Gun (i.S.L.).

15 cm. Long Gun.

15 cm. Russian Gun.

15 cm. Heavy Field Howitzer.('13).

15 cm. Heavy Field Howitzer (older pattern).

21 cm. Mortar (old pattern).

30·5 cm. Mortar.

21 cm. Mortar (newer pattern).

or **42 cm. Mortar.**

HARRISON & SONS LITH ST MARTINS LANE W C

ND - #0451 - 270225 - C2 - 208/167/8 - PB - 9781908487902 - Matt Lamination